Charles
Redd
Monographs
in Western
History

Charles Redd Monographs in Western History

No. 6
Thomas G. Alexander, editor
Essays on the American West, 1974-1975

Soc
F
591
E8223

The Charles Redd Monographs in Western History are made possible by a grant from Charles Redd. This grant served as the basis for the establishment of the Charles Redd Center for Western Studies at Brigham Young University.

Center editor: Thomas G. Alexander

LIBRARY
FLORIDA STATE UNIVERSITY
TALLAHASSEE, FLORIDA 32306

NOV 7 1977

PUBLISHED BY
BRIGHAM YOUNG UNIVERSITY PRESS
PROVO, UTAH 84602

ISBN: 0-8425-0896-1
© 1976 by Brigham Young University Press. All rights reserved
Printed in the United States of America
Additional copies of this monograph or other numbers in this series may be purchased by writing to Brigham Young University, Marketing (University Press), 205 UPB, Provo, Utah 84602.
76 .85M 15043

Contents

Introduction	3
The Western Experience of Henry Adams Richard A. Bartlett	5

The Eliza Enigma: The Life and Legend
  of Eliza R. Snow
                          Maureen Ursenbach Beecher
	29

McCarthyism in the Mountains, 1950-1954 F. Ross Peterson	47
Social Accommodation in Utah Clark S. Knowlton	79
Comparative Frontiers: China and the West Paul V. Hyer	109
The Paradox of Mormon Folklore William A. Wilson	127

Essays on
the American West,
1974-1975

Introduction

Presented as part of the Charles Redd Lectures on the American West at Brigham Young University during the 1974-75 academic year, these essays deal with various aspects of Western development. The authors of the articles range through the humanities and social sciences and offer insights into such diverse aspects of the Western experience as social accommodation, politics, folklore, biography, and comparative development. If one insight emerges from the collection, it is the diversity of the Western experience. It is probable, for instance, that in spite of Henry Adams's interest in medieval Christianity he and Eliza R. Snow would have had little in common. Nevertheless, their experiences are different aspects of the same story.

The Western Experience of Henry Adams
Richard A. Bartlett

Historians have long known that Henry Adams's interests ranged from the administrations of Jefferson and Madison to the cathedrals of medieval France. In this essay, Richard A. Bartlett, professor of history at Florida State University at Tallahassee and author of <u>The New Country: A Social History of the American Frontier, 1776-1890</u>, explains why Adams's inquisitive dilettantism did not lead him to insights into the American West beyond scenery and local color. Bartlett persuasively argues that the assumptions Adams learned from his aristocratic New England background form the basis for this failing. Though Adams traveled in the West and had brothers and friends who were acquainted with the West, none of this interaction provided the catalyst for a perceptive treatment of the significance of the region to national development. Carrying Bartlett's insights a bit further, we may well find that a perceptive understanding of any subject requires an intense period of committed involvement. This may be why Turner, who grew up on the Wisconsin frontier, could develop the "Turner Thesis" and why it passed Adams by.

Interspersed through the pages of history are a few "men for all times," men whose lives are as interesting to us now as they were to their contemporaries, men whose lives and works will fascinate and influence the thoughts of others as long as civilization lasts.

Such a rare man was Henry Brooks Adams. Born in Quincy, Massachusetts, in 1838, he grew up with the knowledge that he was an Adams, the fourth generation of a family which had produced two presidents, John and John Quincy Adams, and a notable American minister to England during the Civil War, Charles Francis Adams, Henry's father.

Henry was one of five children. He had three brothers, John Quincy II, Brooks, and Charles Francis, Jr., and a sister, Louisa, who died in 1870. The boys were educated in the best Adams-Boston-Quincy tradition. All attended Harvard. As for Henry, he stood somewhat apart from his brothers for a reason which has perhaps not been sufficiently emphasized. He was only 5 feet 3 inches tall, his stunted growth probably the result of a siege of scarlet fever when he was a child.[1]

In 1858 he graduated from Harvard and during the next two years he was in Europe doing some studying of German but mostly involved in what was called "the Grand Tour." Home again, he flirted with the profession of law, contemplating setting himself up as a young barrister in St. Louis, but nothing came of this. He did some writing and then, with the coming of the Civil War, sailed for England as his father's private secretary. He again indulged in writing as a secret correspondent for the New York Times. It was in 1862, in a letter to Charles Francis, Jr., who was an officer on active duty in the war, that Henry Adams revealed his prophetic abilities. "Man has mounted science and is now run away with," he wrote. "I firmly believe that before many centuries more, science will be the master of man. The engines he will have invented will be beyond his strength to control. Some day science may have the existence of mankind in its power, and the human race commit suicide by blowing up the world."[2]

At war's end he returned to the United States, indulged in liberal Republican politics, and did some more writing. In 1870 he accepted the position of assistant professor of history at Harvard. He taught medieval history and edited the North American Review. In 1872 he married Marian Hooper, daughter of a prominent Boston physician. Then in the autumn of 1877 he severed his ties with Harvard and moved to Washington. He and his wife, Marian (or Clover, as he called her), established themselves as social aristocrats there, living on "H" Street overlooking Lafayette Square and beyond it the White House. Here conversation and friendships bloomed while Henry, with no classes to meet, childless, and of independent means, produced two biographies, one of John Randolph and one of Albert Gallatin, and two novels, Democracy and Esther, and began writing his nine-volume History of the United States during the Administrations of Jefferson and Madison, though they were not published until the years 1888-91.

The great tragedy in Adams's life, his wife's suicide, took place in 1885. From her death until his own at age eighty in 1918 Henry Adams traveled widely, corresponded with dozens

of prominent men and women, studied and wrote.³ He became an
authority on the history of Tahiti and wrote a book about it;⁴
he knew more about the Cuban insurrection than most officials
in Washington; and he became fascinated with thirteenth-century
Europe. In 1904 he printed Mont-Saint-Michel and Chartres. He
was intrigued by science and the possibility that scientific
laws could be applied to the history of man. The results of
his interest in science and its application to history culmin-
ated in his essays "The Tendency of History" in 1904, "The
Rule of Phase Applied to History" in 1909, and "A Letter to
American Teachers of History" in 1910.⁵ In 1907 he printed
The Education of Henry Adams, an Autobiography. As with his
Mont-Saint-Michel, this was first printed privately.⁶

Adams was so incredibly complex that this brief sketch
cannot do him justice. He has no counterpart in American
life. He was a wealthy dilettante, and as he traveled and
wrote letters, biography, history, philosophies of history, or
even autobiography, his was a giant intellect at work. Let
there be no question of his brilliance. He was also fond of
women, and for more than two decades carried on a platonic
(we assume) love affair with Elizabeth Cameron, the lovely,
well-educated wife of Senator Don Cameron of Pennsylvania.

Yet one of the many themes running through Adams's letters,
and especially through his great book The Education of Henry
Adams, is the theme of failure. He seems to be saying that
he was not educated for the new era, that all his standards
were passé. Some have suggested that he may have taken this
attitude because he was a dilettante in a land where hard work
and the Protestant ethic were standard. Others insist that
this was but a façade, and they point out that Adams always
made it clear that if *he* was ignorant of something, or unpre-
pared for something, so was everybody else.⁷ Many authorities
insist that it is preposterous that so brilliant a man with
such a catholic mind could be considered a failure. He was
so prolific in his writing and such an authority on Tahitian
history and thirteenth-century stained glass, on Cuban insur-
rectionists and the Burr conspiracy, and on the second law of
thermodynamics and force, unity, and multiplicity in history,
that failure seems never to have been within his capacity as
a historian.

But it was on this point, more specifically as an American
historian, that Adams by his own criteria was a failure. True,
his History was well received and is considered a classic today, yet in the first ten years after its publication it earned
him hardly $5,000.⁸ He had hoped to see it sell as well as
the writings of George Bancroft or Francis Parkman, but it fell
far short. His essays applying scientific laws to history were
politely received by the profession, and indeed in 1894 he was

president of the American Historical Association, but the profession, having received his "Rule of Phase" and "A Letter to American Teachers of History," then proceeded to ignore them.

What may have hurt even more was the realization that other thinkers were publishing treatises which excited their colleagues, and that one established a thesis which dominated American historiography for two generations. This intellectual activity came out of the American West or was concerned with that vast area. But Adams gave short shrift to the West in his writings. Somehow he failed to catch the vision, to sense the great sweep of the American people westward as the mighty epic that it really was.

He was not alone in this failure. Many students of nineteenth-century American history have bristled at the failure of George Bancroft, Jared Sparks, John Bach McMaster, James Ford Rhodes, as well as Henry Adams, to give the Westward Movement its due. Of all these men Adams, with his brilliant intellect, his late nineteenth- and early twentieth-century view, should have sensed it. To determine why he failed to do so, let us examine his own Western experience. The investigation divides into three parts:

1. What did Adams actually see of the American West?

2. What did his brothers with whom he was on close terms see of the West?

3. Who were his Western friends?

The answers to these questions should help us better understand Adams's failure.

His Western experience really began in 1871 when Adams was thirty-three years old. One of his friends from Quincy days, Samuel Franklin Emmons, had become a geologist and a member of the Fortieth Parallel Survey.[9] By 1871 this government-financed geological and geographical survey, which was exploring approximately the region along the Union Pacific-Central Pacific railroads from the Rockies to the Sierras, was into its fifth year.[10] Emmons invited Adams, who had puttered around with geology a bit, to accompany him "on one of the field-parties in summer."[11]

Adams felt ready for the change. He was about to put to bed the July issue of the North American Review, and he was faced with the grading of examination papers. As any professor knows, exam time in June, at the end of nine months of students and faculty committee meetings, is trying indeed.

"It would be fun to send you some of my examination papers," Adams wrote to his British friend Charles Milnes Gaskell. "My rule in making them is to ask questions which I myself can't answer. . . ."[12] He went on to describe his projected vacation. "I shall at once start on an expedition which will lead me for the next six weeks into paths unknown to European blokes," he wrote. One of his friends (Emmons) had invited him "to go with his party on an expedition down the cañon of the Green River. . . . If you have a modern atlas you may find the district not far from Salt Lake and the Mormons. . . . I shall not be back within reach of mankind before the 1st of September, and my next letter to you may perhaps be written from a country wilder than anything in Siberia."[13]

On July 8 he left Boston, arriving four days later in Cheyenne. There he inadvertently bumped into Clarence King, the head of the Survey, and, discovering that the Survey was divided into two parts, grabbed a place with the unit that was just getting started. Claiming that he spurned tents, preferring to sleep under the sky "for the purpose of studying sunrises," Adams appears to have entered into the rugged life with gusto. "I was given a big black mule," he wrote, "and got a little rifle which I hung at my saddle-bow. I put on a flannel shirt, leather breeches and big leggins, and having climbed to the top of the mule I proceeded to career across the country mostly at a slow walk, climb mountains where my hair stood on end, and shoot at rabbits and antelopes with enthusiasm if not with success."[14]

He enjoyed the rugged life immensely, living in the open at six to twelve thousand feet, satisfying a voracious appetite. And it was with this unit of the Survey that Adams found himself in Estes Park, Colorado. He wrote in the <u>Education</u> that

> he liked to wander off alone on his mule, and pass the day fishing at a mountain stream or exploring a valley. One morning, when the party was camped high above Estes Park, on the flank of Long's Peak, he borrowed a rod, and rode down over a rough trail into Estes Park, for some trout. The day was fine, and hazy with the smoke of forest fires a thousand miles away; the park stretched its English beauties off to the base of its bordering mountains in natural landscape and archaic peace; the stream was just fishy enough to tempt lingering along its banks. Hour after hour the sun moved westward and the fish moved eastward, or disappeared altogether, until at last when the fisherman cinched his mule, sunset was nearer than he thought. Darkness caught him before he could catch his trail. Not caring to tumble into

some fifty foot hole, he 'allowed' he was lost, and turned back. In half an hour he was out of the hills, and under the stars of Estes Park, but he saw no prospect of supper or bed.[15]

Eastern dude he was to be sure, but he possessed the common sense to let the mule find its way in the darkness. In a couple of hours "a light showed in the distance," and he found a cabin and human company. His good fortune was with him, for one of the inhabitants was Clarence King. King was a New Englander, a graduate of the Sheffield Scientific School at Yale. "In the cabin luxury provided a room and one bed for guests. They shared the room and the bed, and talked till far towards dawn."[16]

Later that summer Adams went from the rather settled area of north-central Colorado westward to Fort Bridger, in the midst of "an awful wilderness of alkili desert covered with low sagebrushes. . . . Here," he wrote Gaskell, "everything is wild enough to suit me, and I have no nearer neighbors than the Mormons, about one hundred and fifty miles to the westward." From there he joined the party in the field and explored the Uintah Mountains, fished for trout, and even noted that "here is a wild Indian--a Shoshone--just riding up to the door of my tent and silently watching me as I write. . . . On the whole I think I shall leave this country in possession of the noble savage without a pang. He may wander at will in the alkili for all me."[17]

Autumn came, and Adams returned to Harvard. He had enjoyed his trip, only disparaging Colorado to the extent that "it does not approach Switzerland," and described his Uintah trip as "a stunner," saying that he "enjoyed the life and learned a deal about his own country, and forgot all the history I had studied for a year."[18]

Not for fifteen years would Adams again travel into the trans-Mississippi West. In that time he married, quit his Harvard professorship, and settled in Washington, D.C. He had written two novels and two biographies, edited Gallatin's papers, and started on his great History, and his wife had taken her own life before he went west again.

On 3 June 1886 he left Boston for Japan accompanied by the artist John La Farge. They rode west in regal splendor in the directors' private car of the Union Pacific Railroad, of which his brother Charles was then president. He found San Francisco looking "as though its glories had passed, . . . a little seedy." On their return five months later the city looked "improved." They ran down to Monterey, where, he wrote, "the Cliff House [described by his friend King as "that Ultima Thule of the Aryan migration"[19]] is seedy, but the seals still grunt."[20] A few days later Charles Francis Adams, Jr., met them at San Francisco and accompanied them home via the southern route, passing through the Mojave desert, Albuquerque, and St. Joseph.[21] If the trip across the continent made any impression upon Adams, that impression does not appear in any of his published writings or letters.

Two years later, in October and November 1888, he toured the Far West with Sir Robert Cunliffe, a British friend. Adams enjoyed the trip immensely, traveling west in private U.P. Car 010. They stopped at Salt Lake--by which he probably meant the city--and then traveled north. "You should have seen us two animated dust heaps driving across twenty-five miles of fluid dust and solid lava to see Shoshone Falls," he wrote Elizabeth Cameron.[22] After clambering about the Falls he also reported that his "legs ached for a week, and [his] very hat stood on end with terror."

They went down the Columbia by steamer, saw Portland and Mt. Shasta, and arrived in San Francisco, "dull in spite of its swell club-house. . . ." From there they journeyed to Yosemite and the big trees. "I have just returned from a long day in the mountains," Adams wrote to Mrs. Cameron, "where fresh snow was about us, and where I felt myself a modified though deteriorated, black bear, with strong prejudices about civilization." They returned East by way of the southern route and New Orleans.[23]

In 1890 the little dilettante again traveled west in the company of John La Farge, embarking from San Francisco for a two-year tour in the South Seas and eventually around the world.[24] Finally, from mid-July to mid-September 1894, Adams vacationed in Yellowstone Park and the Tetons. This was in a year of severe economic depression in which for a time the Adams family fortune was in jeopardy--the year of the Pullman strike and the year after the repeal of the Sherman Silver Purchase Act. Adams planned this trip as a much-needed vacation, taking with him his very close friend John Hay and Hay's son Del; Joseph Paxton Iddings, a geologist; and W. Hallett Phillips, a young lawyer from Washington, D.C., who was considered the leader of the group. Their guide was a capable Westerner named Billy Hofer.[25]

Adams spent five weeks in the wilderness of southern Yellowstone Park and on down into the Tetons. Writing to Elizabeth Cameron from Upper Geyser Basin Camp, 29 July 1894, he said,

> To me the chief pleasure is absence of other life, and a sense of daily action; forest, sky, and running water without a house to be seen for a month; pleasant companions and no special thoughts. The drawbacks are flies

> and mosquitoes; wet weather and cold; fatigue
> and down-timber; glaring geyser basins and
> wet feet. . . . At half past six this morning,
> it was 39 degrees in my tent, and I thought
> the night the coldest I ever felt; but I had
> a bath of hot geyser-water in my tent, and
> Lucullus never invented a more delicious one,
> if he gave his mind to the bath-business. The
> mosquitoes are infernal, but even they can't
> go the nights, and retire to their fur night-
> bags long before I crawl into mine. . . .
> We strike into the wild country to the
> southward tomorrow, and cut out our last ties
> to stage-coaches and roads. If all goes well,
> you will not hear from me for another month.
> Little as I care for these gamy pleasures which
> could give new life to our Teddy, I am at least
> contented to be here. . . ."[26] [The "Teddy" was
> obviously Theodore Roosevelt.]

On September 1 the party emerged from the mountains and arrived at Mammoth Hot Springs; later they traveled north another sixty miles to catch the Northern Pacific trains at Livingston, Montana. Writing from there, Adams described the outing as consisting of riding "three or four hundred miles on Indian ponies over trails which may suit elk, but are not adapted to rapid transit." He described Yellowstone's scenery as being "not remarkably fine. Except for the Grand Canyon, it is rather a bore." But he found the Two Ocean Pass country and the Tetons different, original, and "superb."[27] After twenty-two camps and a diet of elk meat and trout, Adams conceded that Hay had "become a blooming mountaineer, and I--remain, as Phillips insists, a dude."[28]

Later in his _Education_ Adams said of the Yellowstone trip that

> he found there little to study. The Geysers
> were an old story; the Snake River posed no
> vital statistics except in its fordings; even
> the Tetons were as calm as they were lovely;
> while the wapiti and bear, innocent of strikes
> and corners, laid no traps. . . . Compared with
> the Rockies in 1871, the sense of wilderness
> had vanished; one saw no possible adventures
> except to break one's neck as in chasing an
> aniseed fox."[29]

Sad news awaited him when he emerged from the wilderness. His eldest brother, John Quincy II, had died on August 14. What to do? Why go home if a brother is already dead and buried? Hay and the rest of the party had already entrained for the East. "I am alone, and as I have a month to spare, I turn westward again, with only a general idea where I may bring up," Adams wrote to his friend Edward William Hooper. "My first stop will be Seattle. I may go to Alaska. I may go home by the Canadian Pacific. Anyway I have no address, and my letters stay at Washington. No one can want me, but by October 1 I shall probably appear at the Knickerbocker Club [in New York City]."30

From Livingston he journeyed just about as he said he would into the Pacific Northwest. He returned East for a short while and then headed for Mexico, the Gulf, and the Caribbean, finally coming to rest in Washington, D.C., in April 1895. "He was beginning to think," he wrote in his Education, "that he knew enough about the edges of life--tropical islands, mountain solitudes, archaic law, and retrograde types. Infinitely more amusing and incomparably more picturesque than civilization, they educated only artists, and, as one's sixtieth year approached, the artist began to die. . . ."31

As far as I can determine, Adams never went into the Far West again. He had attended the Chicago Exposition in 1893 and would visit the St. Louis Exposition of 1904, however; to him these trips may have been considered "trips west," since anything west of the Alleghenies was "West" to him.32 His Western experience insofar as his travels are concerned consisted, then, of three vacations, one in 1871, one in 1888, and one in 1894. He traveled in the West in 1886 and again in 1890, but these trips were parts of longer journeys to the South Seas and the Orient; and he attended the World's Fairs of 1893 and 1904. Altogether in his life of eighty years rather less than six months were spent by Henry Adams in the American West.

A second aspect of Adams's Western experience was through his family contacts. These were restricted primarily to just one of his brothers, Charles Francis, who pursued a business career and was president of the Union Pacific Railroad from 1884 until 1890. Charles Francis had first seen the West as far as Lawrence, Kansas, on a political tour in 1860, and he was fascinated by what he had seen.33

After the Civil War he invested in copper mines in Michigan and silver mines in Nevada and Colorado, depending for his advice upon Clarence King, Samuel Franklin Emmons, and well-known mining authority Rossiter W. Raymond. Charles Francis invested in railroads in Michigan as well as in the big Western roads such as the Burlington, the Santa Fe, the Rio Grande, and of course the Union Pacific. And he sensed the future greatness of Westport-Landing, now Kansas City, Missouri, and invested heavily there--especially in the stockyards, "the linchpin of the Adams fortune."[34] He also invested heavily on the Kansas side of the Kaw, and his Kaw Valley Town Site and Bridge Company divided up over 400 percent on its capital by 1900. In one year, 1885, it paid forty percent dividends; and in 1886 twelve monthly dividends of ten percent a month.

Charles Francis Adams traveled extensively, investing in stockyards and land in Denver, Fort Worth, San Antonio, Houston, Salt Lake City, Portland, Seattle, Helena, Spokane, and Lewiston. He was, he said, "practically betting on the growth of the country."[35] From 1870 until 1890 he went west at least once every year, some of his trips lasting for months and covering ten thousand miles. "He knew the West at first hand but he detested it," writes his biographer. Adams referred to it as "that great, fat, uninteresting West," the fascination of 1860 having disappeared after dozens of lonely nights in Western hotels and greasy meals in Western restaurants. On his return east from these trips he liked to celebrate by quaffing a bottle of champagne as soon as he smelled the salt air of the Atlantic, even if it was at New York City.[36]

The feeling was reciprocal: Westerners did not particularly like him. He was certainly one of those "bunko men of Boston" mentioned by a Nebraska senator while criticizing the Union Pacific management.[37] Yet after he left the presidency of the railroad and had weathered the financial storms of the 1890s, Charles Francis turned to the writing of history and, in a speech honoring the dedication of the building to house the Wisconsin Historical Society, he gave a talk entitled "The Sifted Grain and the Grain Sifters," in which he applied Darwinism to the westward movement. It had no known effect upon the thinking of his brother Henry, if Henry even bothered to read it.[38]

The most eccentric of the fourth generation of Adamses, yet with flashes of brilliance, was brother Brooks. Born in 1848, he was ten years younger than Henry. Within a week after graduation from Harvard in 1870 he and two classmates began a grand tour of the West: to St. Paul by train, down the Mississippi by stern-wheeler to St. Louis, then by rail to San Francisco, Yosemite, and then Salt Lake City. There Brooks, letting himself be identified as son of the American minister to England during the Civil War who had aided Mormon emigrants, was warmly entertained by the Saints and met Brigham Young. He went to Denver, then on horses into the Ute country in the Rockies to the West.[39] Brooks's subsequent travels are, as one would expect of an eccentric, difficult to follow, but certainly

the West left little impression on him. As for the other
Adams, John Quincy II, he occasionally traveled in the West
with his brother Charles Francis but, though likeable and
sociable, made the smallest mark of the Adams boys. In sum
there is no indication that the Western experience of his brothers had any effect upon Adams's thinking.

A third category of his Western experience concerns Adams's
friends who were either Westerners themselves or were men whose
interests, some of them at least, lay in the West. There were
a number of such individuals with whom he corresponded frequently and met often. Surely they contributed to Adams's
knowledge of the West and are therefore of importance.

First and foremost of these men was Clarence King. Like
Adams, the geologist was short of stature and balding; unlike
Adams, he had a tendency toward obesity. King seemed to Adams
the perfectly educated man for the age. Adams appears to have
envied him because King--self-confident, capable, ambitious,
a scientist in an age that idolized science--was everything
Adams wished he could be. The geologist was also a delightful
conversationalist, a dilettante whose excesses, including the
lavish spending of other people's money, continual travel,
and a secret life involving his common-law marriage to a black
woman by whom he had several children, certainly made of him
a most fascinating friend. "He knew more than Adams did of
art and poetry," one reads in the Education. "He knew America,
especially west of the hundredth meridian, better than any
one. . . . He knew even women; even the American woman; even
the New York woman, which was saying much."[40]

King possessed some literary ability, though it has probably been overrated. He published some articles which were
later to constitute a volume entitled Mountaineering in the
Sierra Nevada, which Adams reviewed, as he also did King's own
volume of the Fortieth Parallel Survey Reports, "Systematic
Geology."[41]

But what influence had King upon the thought and writings
of Henry Adams? If anything, a negative influence within the
framework of Adams's works on American history. King was not
by birth a Westerner; he was a New England blueblood who, as
a professional geologist, spent much time in the West. He was
director of the United States Geological Exploration of the
Fortieth Parallel, the exposer of the Great Diamond Hoax and,
in later years, an investor in Western cattle ranching and
mining enterprises. He was a mining consultant for wealthy
investors.[42] But there is little in his writings to indicate
that he possessed a "sense of history" involving the westward
movement. King was a polished raconteur, a cosmopolitan man-on-the-go, and Adams and his wife Marian delighted in King's
great tales of the West. But tall tales are not sound history.

Ever searching for fortune, the geologist died in Phoenix, Arizona, 24 December 1901, leaving a massive indebtedness to both Adams and John Hay.[43] King was a failure; he ran neither his financial affairs nor his personal life with honor, strictly speaking, and his accomplishments as a geologist, especially his theories about catastrophism, have been discarded. Contrary to the opinion of Bernard De Voto, who said that Adams was "a literary person of considerably inferior intelligence [to King's],"[44] Clarence King was not as intelligent as Henry Adams; neither was Bernard De Voto, for that matter.

Adams had other friends in the realms of geology and paleontology. He had studied under Louis Agassiz at Harvard, and for all his life agreed with Agassiz in his rejection of Darwin's theories. He had met the geologist Sir Charles Lyell in England; he knew Arnold and James D. Hague, Joseph Paxton Iddings, and Samuel Franklin Emmons of the Geological Survey; and he had conversed with Major John Wesley Powell, the geologist of the Colorado River.[45] In a general way these men undoubtedly influenced Adams in his thinking about science, but from the point of view of his writings in American history, they had slight influence upon him.

A second friend considered by Adams as a Westerner was John Hay. Born in 1838, the same year as Adams, of frontier stock in Indiana, Hay grew up in Warsaw and Springfield, Illinois, but graduated in 1858 from Brown University in Providence, Rhode Island. Subsequently he read law in Lincoln's law office; later he became Lincoln's assistant private secretary. Then in March 1865 he accepted the position of secretary of legation at Paris, and for the next five years spent most of his time overseas, in Vienna and finally in Madrid. In 1870 he joined the staff of the New York Tribune and by 1871, having published in Atlantic, Harper's Monthly, and Harper's Weekly, he had become nationally known. Hay wrote local color, his best known characters being "Little Breeches" and "Jim Bludsoe." Those two became as well known to his generation as L'il Abner and Snuffy Smith to ours. Hay's Pike County Ballads and Other Pieces would shortly appear. He won his initial fame through his writings.

Hay married well and settled in Cleveland where his wife's inheritance made him rich. He invested well and became a man of affairs in business. And so we have here a most complex man, a man of letters--he is also well known as the author, along with John Nicolay, of a distinguished biography of Lincoln--a man of the business world, and a man in public life, for eventually he served as secretary of state under both McKinley and Theodore Roosevelt.

He had met Adams as early as the Great Secession winter of 1860-61, had conversed with him occasionally during the war years, and by the 1880s Adams considered Hay, along with King, as one of his closest friends. Add Marian Adams and Hay's wife, Clara Louise, and we have the Five of Hearts, a group of close friends so attached that they had a tea service made just for their meetings.[46]

Hay came out of what Adams considered the West, but as Hay's biographer emphasizes, "Hay was not a politician and, in spite of his origins, not a pioneer."[47] His writing, save for his Lincoln biography, was about a backwash type of American pioneer, the Pike County illiterate; the name is from Pike County, Missouri, but in a larger sense includes characteristics of the settlers of southern Missouri and northern Arkansas. Hay's literary contribution was the Pike County local color and lingo and tall stories. He never appears to have grasped the massiveness of the Westward Movement, which during his lifetime nearly brought about the completion of the contiguous forty-eight states; at the time of his birth in 1838, there had been just twenty-six.

Other friends of Adams who were either born in the West or shared in the Western experience do not loom as molders of opinion, for Adams did not see much of them. One was Bret Harte, a man to whom Adams took a distinct liking.[48] But again, Harte's portrayal of mining camp life in the Far West never rose above descriptions of social life, local color, and lingo. Moreover, Harte was New York born, did not go west until he was nineteen, and fled from there as soon as his income warranted it. Adams knew and admired Francis Parkman, but Parkman in his single work on the westward movement, The Oregon Trail, failed to grasp the significance of the movement; he looked down his Yankee nose at the uncouth Oregonians. Adams knew Theodore Roosevelt, but did not admire him. And rather curiously, he appears never to have met Mark Twain.[49]

Such was Henry Adams's Western experience. He saw the West from the tourist's point of view and never appears to have contemplated the historical implications of what he witnessed and experienced. His family connections certainly involved discussions about the West, but Charles Francis, who had the most interests out there, detested it. And Adams's friends who participated in the Western experience narrated local color, local lingo, and Western tall tales. In a word, the Western experience of Henry Adams was shallow.

This is not presented as a criticism but merely as a fact. However, even if his travels were in the nature of vacations, we must remember that thought does not stop on such occasions, and the historian can no more cease contemplating thoughts of history than can a vacationing Catholic priest ignore the once-a-day Mass. But Henry Adams saw no great lessons in his Western experience, no great spectacles worth writing about,

while among his contemporaries in the intellectual community
much thinking and writing were being done. Moreover, it was
noticed; it had an effect. Four examples of men who were impressed by the West they saw and whose thoughts were molded or
inspired by the Western experience are James Bryce, Charles
Howard Shinn, Henry George, and Frederick Jackson Turner.
   The first of these men, Viscount James Bryce, was an Adams
acquaintance. In his great work The American Commonwealth,
first published in 1888, Bryce devoted considerable space to
the westward movement, the Westerner, and the meaning of that
vast area in American history. He analyzed the "character and
temper of the men, . . . for the West," he emphasized, "is the
most American part of America." Or again, he wrote, "These
[Western] people are intoxicated by the majestic scale of the
nature in which their lot is cast, . . . they gild their own
struggles for fortune with the belief that they are the missionaries of civilization and the instruments of Providence in
the greatest work the world has seen. . . ."[50] Bryce was no
uncouth Westerner, but an English gentleman who crowded into a
single lifetime the roles of world traveler, historian, and
diplomat. He was at home in the medieval Germanies, in his own
London, or in America. Adams must have cringed at the list of
his accomplishments.
   A second historian who should have influenced Adams, and
who was influenced by the West, was a late-blooming Californian, Charles Howard Shinn. He entered the new Johns Hopkins
University as a special student when he was thirty years old,
and there fell under the influence of Herbert Baxter Adams
(no relation to the Boston Adamses), a noted political scientist-historian who had earned his Ph.D. at Heidelberg. Herbert
Baxter Adams subscribed to the "germ theory" that the democratic processes had originated among Teutonic peoples in the forests of Europe and in an unbroken stream had crossed to Anglo-Saxon England; and from there, having developed for several
centuries, the concepts were brought to the British colonies
in the New World.[51]
   Charles Shinn saw the gold and silver mining era in the Far
West as a chapter in this progressive history of the Germanic
peoples. Again and again he pointed out similarities between
Germanic customs, such as practices among the miners in the
Harz mountains, and the customs that sprouted in American mining camps. To us today the whole theory seems ridiculous, but
it did not appear that way a century ago, and its defenders
did contribute to the acceptance of the scientific approach to
history.
   What did the historian Adams have to say about Shinn's
book, Mining Camps: A Study in American Frontier Government?
Apparently nothing. Yet in 1876, eight years prior to Shinn's

book, Adams had published Essays in Anglo-Saxon Law, which he had edited and the first of which he authored, his students writing the others.[52] In these papers the attempt was made to link Germanic practices with medieval Anglo-Saxon law in England. One might think that he would have been intrigued by Shinn's monograph, possibly even piqued that such a study involving the Teutonic theory should appear about an American development, written by a far less well-educated historian than he. But we find not a word.

In 1879 an obscure newspaper man named Henry George tried to answer the problem of abundance and wealth on the one hand and of poverty on the other. He accomplished this to his satisfaction in his great work Progress and Poverty. It was widely read both here and abroad. John Dewey said that "no man . . . has a right to consider himself an educated man in social thought unless he has some first-hand acquaintance with the theoretical contribution of this great American thinker."[53] George had lived in San Francisco during the decade 1858-68, and there, as his admirer George Bernard Shaw said, he witnessed "the growth of the whole tragedy of civilization from the primitive forest clearing."[54] But if either Henry Adams or his brother Brooks, who was even more interested in economics, paid any attention to--or even bothered to read--Progress and Poverty, it does not appear in their writings or published letters.

Finally, at the meeting of the American Historical Association held at the World's Columbian Exposition in Chicago, an American from the Middle West read a paper that, as we all know, had a decisive effect upon American historiography. This was, of course, Frederick Jackson Turner's "Significance of the Frontier in American History," which found in the existence of an area of free land and a moving frontier an American interpretation for American history. Turner later met Adams, but there is no indication that the little Boston brahmin was impressed, or that Turner was impressed with him.[55]

Yet if Adams failed to appreciate the greatness of the American achievement, this is not to say that he was unaware of it. His historian's mind at work is clearly apparent when he writes of his impressions of the two great fairs, the first at Chicago in 1893 and the second at St. Louis in 1904. In his mind these expositions were "in the West," and his comments show how he approached the great questions, the great conundrums of history. He visited the Chicago Exposition twice, traveling alone the second time and spending a fortnight there.[56]

That summer season of 1893 his active mind was concerned over the condition of the Adams family fortune, the depression, and the silver question. In his Education he reveals a concern over the seemingly chaotic condition of society, a fear that, as he said, "something new and curious was about to happen in the world. Great changes had taken place since 1870 in the forces at work; the old machine ran far behind its duty; somewhere--somehow--it was bound to break down, and if it happened to break precisely over one's head, it gave the better chance for study."57 By implication the machine had broken over Adams's head--his fortune teetered on the brink for awhile-- and the Chicago Exposition seemed to add unfathomable mysteries to the chaos of the time. It "defied philosophy"; he found its mere existence "more surprising, as it was, than anything else on the continent, Niagara Falls, the Yellowstone Geysers, and the whole railway system thrown in." He finally stated that "Chicago [and probably he meant the city as well as its fair] was the first expression of American thought as unity; one must start there."58

Eleven years later, in 1904, he visited the St. Louis Exposition and again proclaimed astonishment that "a third-rate town of half-a-million people without history, education, unity, or art, and with little capital--[was] doing what London, Paris, or New York would have shrunk from attempting." He and John Hay, with whom he traveled to the fair, passed from Pittsburgh through Ohio and Indiana, amazed at the chimneys and smoke, "dirty suburbs filled with scrap-iron, scrap-paper, and cinders." He added, "Adams thought the Secretary of State should have rushed to the platform at every station to ask who were the people; for the American of the prime seemed to be extinct with the Shawnee and the buffalo."59

Instead he found "Germans and Slavs, or whatever their race-names, who had overflowed these regions as though the Rhine and the Danube had turned their floods into the Ohio. . . . Within less than thirty years," he wrote, "this mass of mixed humanities, brought together by steam, was squeezed and welded into approach to shape, a product of so much mechanical power, and bearing no distinctive marks, but the pressure. . . ."60

Such was Henry Adams's view of the West, that massive hinterland west of the Appalachians or the Berkshires. He saw its mountain heights, dusty deserts, and scenes of grandeur such as the falls of Yosemite or the Grand Canyon of the Yellowstone, but read no lessons, much less an education; they were for artists. And he witnessed the transition of the Middle West in the score of years from the early seventies to the nineties, or even to the turn of the century, but his reaction was one of bewilderment. Who were these people? What had happened to peaceful, agrarian America? He seems to have suffered from future shock, nineteenth-century vintage. He witnessed the pollution of steam-powered industry, which had

transformed so much of the land from agricultural to industrial
production and had brought a Babel of races by steamboat and
steam train into the Mississippi valley. He granted that
these people were being "squeezed and welded" into shape, but
denied them any distinction save signs of the pressures under
which they worked and lived. They were not the old Americans
who "seemed to be extinct with the Shawnee and the buffalo."
He gave them no credit for becoming worthwhile Americans just
as good as the American prime.

His was a pessimistic view. It said nothing good about
the Americanization of these people, of their acceptance of the
whole spectrum of values and hopes and fears that made up the
American psyche. It barely hinted at the abilities of these
atoms of a new society to govern themselves and live lives of
fulfillment and joy. Adams saw nothing but puzzlement and
chaos: of the Chicago Exposition, "one could still explain
nothing that needed explanation," he wrote.[61] Baffled by it
all, Adams sat down "beneath the steps of Richard Hunt's
dome"[62] and tried to figure it all out.

Yet it was at this same exposition that a young historian
out of the West delivered a paper that exalted the American
accomplishment, credited the westward movement with the cre-
ation of an American character, and evinced optimism, verve,
hope, even adventure in nearly every sentence.

But Adams's History was of the old school that viewed
history as past politics and politics as present history. He
gave short shrift to Lewis and Clark and Zebulon Pike. He did
not even mention the explorations of Sir William Dunbar and
George Hunter, or Thomas Freeman.[63] John Jacob Astor was barely mentioned and Astoria not at all. That there was a West,
that America's star lay westward, that Americans were a people
elevated above the level of Europeans Adams granted. But Westerners were uncouth to him, eye gougers and nose biters and
carousers.[64]

It is here, one suspects, that Adams's failure is explained.
The Westward movement was primarily a folk movement of the
hard-working and ambitious poor. Adams the aristocrat, the
Boston brahmin, independently wealthy and of the New England
"establishment," did not understand the westward-moving American people. Hopes, aspirations, the very real problems of
bringing acres into cultivation, breeding cattle, building
houses, missed him completely. As an aristocrat who never had
to worry about mortgage payments or money to purchase seed,
livestock, or even the food for his family, he passed off the
westward-moving American people as ants or bees; he denigrated
them. Adams chose to look eastward to Europe or else concentrate on the America that lay east of the Appalachians in the
early nineteenth century. He would have nothing to do with

the respectable, hard-working poor who advanced west.
    Another reason for his failure as an American historian was his dilettantism. He wrote of the United States, 1801-17, because it intrigued him, not because there was a great market for such a study. He wrote biographies of Randolph and Gallatin because they interested him and he wrote two novels because the challenge amused him. He wrote of Tahiti; then he fell in love with medieval Europe and came up with <u>Mont-Saint-Michel and Chartres</u>. Then, in that age when science was sacred, he decided that history was also subject to absolute scientific laws. So he pursued chemistry and physics and the second law of thermodynamics and entropy, finally writing "The Rule of Phase in History" and "A Letter to American Teachers of History." The history profession simply rejected his far-off ideas, though honoring him, as it later honored his brother Charles Francis, with the presidency of the American Historical Association. Henry's writings got so far out that his Pulitzer prize-winning biographer, Ernest Samuels, ends a lengthy critique of chapters thirty-three and thirty-four of the <u>Education</u> ("A Dynamic Theory of History" and "A Law of Acceleration") by writing that "they stand as a monument to intellectual ambition, or the most prodigious tale of a tub by which a supreme ironist defies reason to pursue him."[65] Rather than follow the trends of American historiography, Adams struck out on lonesome trails. He paid for his independence.
    A dilettante in the forest of intellectuality was Henry Adams, pursuing only the whims that crept into his brilliant mind. He was both above the heads of the American people and apart from their lines of interest. This is not to condemn either his great <u>History</u> or his theories. In an age when scholars considered all history as past politics, Adams's <u>History</u> was a great contribution. He applied scientific methods of research, made wide use of archival sources, and wrote with a lucid pen about diplomacy and politics. His was, as Henry Steele Commager says, the last and the best of the old style histories;[66] just a few years after the final volume was published in 1891 American historians led by Turner wrote history from a different and far wider point of view. Great as Adams's <u>History</u> was and is, it did not sell well; and esoteric as were his essays on a theory of history, they were ignored by the mainstream of American historians. Adams failed to move with the mainstream, and so he probably did feel left out, isolated, a failure.
    He chose to move in other directions, and this was his prerogative. But in so doing he worked against the trends of the time, one of which was an increased interest in the American West. It cost him dearly. Had Adams grasped the westward vision, we might be speaking today of an Adams, rather than of a Turner thesis.

REFERENCES

1. There is an enormous amount of material on Henry Adams, but fortunately one work towers above the rest. This is Ernest Samuels's three-volume biography The Young Henry Adams; Henry Adams: The Middle Years; and Henry Adams: The Major Phase (Cambridge, Mass.: The Belknap Press of Harvard University Press, 1958-64). A good brief biography and interpretation is George Hochfield, Henry Adams: An Introduction and Interpretation (New York: Barnes and Noble, Inc., 1962). An earlier biography is James Truslow Adams, Henry Adams (New York: Albert and Charles Boni, 1933). Still another is Elizabeth Stevenson, Henry Adams: A Biography (New York: The Macmillan Company, 1956). Interpretive studies include Timothy Paul Donovan, Henry Adams and Brooks Adams (Norman: University of Oklahoma Press, 1961); Robert A. Hume, Runaway Star: An Appreciation of Henry Adams (New York: Cornell University Press, 1951); William H. Jordy, Henry Adams: Scientific Historian (New Haven: Yale University Press, 1952); and Jacob C. Levinson, The Mind and Art of Henry Adams (Boston: Houghton Mifflin Co., 1957). No student of Adams can ignore his own autobiography, The Education of Henry Adams (New York: The Modern Library, 1931; there are numerous other editions).

2. Worthington Chauncey Ford, ed., A Cycle of Adams Letters, 1861-1865, 2 vols. (London: Constable and Co., Ltd., 1921), 1:135.

3. Among the great sources for the study of Adams are his letters. Two of the best collections are Henry Adams, Letters of Henry Adams, 1858-1918, ed. Worthington Chauncey Ford, 2 vols. (Boston: Houghton Mifflin Co., 1930, 1938); and Henry Adams, Henry Adams and His Friends, ed. Harold Dean Cater (Boston: Houghton Mifflin Co., 1947).

4. Adams printed this short work privately; it has never been published. Its original title was "Memoirs of Marau Taaroa, Last Queen of Tahiti" (1893); he reprinted it as "Memoirs of Arii Taimai E" (1901).

5. The three essays are contained in Henry Adams, The Degradation of the Democratic Dogma, ed. Brooks Adams (New York: The Macmillan Co., 1919).

6. Mont-Saint-Michel and Chartres was first published by Houghton Mifflin Co. (Boston, 1913). It is now available in paperback. The Education was first published by Houghton Mifflin in 1918.

7. The Education is permeated with such comments. An excellent example is the last two pages of Chapter IV, "Harvard College." (This is on pages sixty-eight and sixty-nine of the Modern Library edition [New York, 1931] but in other editions can be readily identified as above.)

8. Samuels, Henry Adams: The Major Phase, 309, 366.

9. Richard A. Bartlett, Great Surveys of the American West (Norman: University of Oklahoma Press, 1962), 148.

10. Ibid., 123-215.

11. Henry Adams, Letters, ed. Ford, 1:211.

12. Ibid.

13. Ibid.

14. Ibid., 213.

15. Adams, Education, 310.

16. Ibid., 311.

17. Henry Adams, Letters, ed. Ford, 1:214.

18. Ibid., 213.

19. Clarence King, The Helmet of Mambrino, intro. Francis P. Farquhar (San Francisco: The Book Club of California, 1938), xix-xx.

20. Henry Adams and His Friends, ed. Cater, 161, 173.

21. Samuels, Henry Adams: The Middle Years, 312.

22. Letters, ed. Ford, 1:395.

23. Ibid.

24. Samuels, Henry Adams: The Major Phase, 41-64.

25. Education, 350.

26. Letters, ed. Ford, II, 54.

27. Henry Adams and His Friends, ed. Cater, 327.

28. Education, 350; Letters, ed. Ford, 2:54-55.

29. Education, 350.

30. Henry Adams and His Friends, ed. Cater, 327.

31. Education, 350-51.

32. Ibid., 339, 465-66.

33. Edward Chase Kirkland, Charles Francis Adams, Jr., 1835-1915: The Patrician at Bay (Cambridge: Harvard University Press, 1965), 20.

34. Ibid., 33.

35. Ibid., 73.

36. Ibid., 75.

37. Ibid., 100.

38. Ibid., 207.

39. Arthur F. Beringause, Brooks Adams (New York: Alfred A. Knopf, 1955), 47.

40. Education, 311. See also David H. Dickinson, "Henry Adams and Clarence King, the Record of a Friendship," New England Quarterly, 17, no. 2 (June, 1944):229-54.

41. Adams reviewed "Systematic Geology" in Nation, January 23, 1879; Mountaineering in the Sierra Nevada in the April 1872 North American Review.

42. Bartlett, Great Surveys, 123-215; Harry Crosby, "So Deep a Trail: A Biography of Clarence King," (Ph.D. diss., Stanford University, 1953).

43. Discussion of King's plight is found in Boxes 28 and 30 of the Emmons Papers, Library of Congress, Washington, D.C.

44. Bernard De Voto, The Year of Decision: 1846 (Boston: Little, Brown and Co., 1943), 348.

45. Samuels, Henry Adams: The Middle Years, 35-37, 39; Henry Adams: The Major Phase, 480; Education, 127, 309-10, 350. These are but a few of many references to these individuals.

46. This thumbnail biography is based upon Tyler Dennett, John Hay: From Poetry to Politics (New York: Dodd, Mead and Co., 1934); for the Five of Hearts, see Samuels, Henry Adams: The Major Phase, 191, 562.

47. Dennett, John Hay, 62.

48. Education, 259, 315, 385; Samuels, Henry Adams: The Major Phase, 166, 345.

49. Samuels, Henry Adams: The Major Phase, 251.

50. James Bryce, The American Commonwealth, 2 vols., 3rd ed. (New York: The Macmillan Co., 1892), 2:830, 833-34.

51. Charles Francis Shinn, Mining Camps: A Study in American Frontier Government, intro. Rodman W. Paul (New York: Harper Torchbooks, 1965), xii.

52. Essays in Anglo-Saxon Law, ed. Henry Adams (Boston: Little, Brown and Co., 1905). This includes his own essay, "The Anglo-Saxon Courts of Law."

53. Quoted in Merle Curti, Willard Thorp, and Carlos Baker, American Issues: The Social Record, 4th ed. (Philadelphia: J. B. Lippincott Co., 1960), 679.

54. Quoted in Daniel Aaron, Men of Good Hope (New York: Oxford University Press, 1951), 62.

55. Samuels, Henry Adams: The Major Phase, 435, 492.

56. Education, 332, 339, 465.

57. Ibid., 338.

58. Ibid., 340, 343.

59. Ibid., 466.

60. Ibid.

61. Ibid., 339.

62. Ibid., 340.

63. Henry Adams, History, 9 vols. (New York: Charles Scribner's Sons, 1888-92), 1:12-13, 213-17.

64. Ibid., 54-55.

65. Samuels, Henry Adams: The Major Phase, 393.

66. Henry Adams, History, intro. Henry Steele Commager, 9 vols. in 4 (New York: Albert and Charles Boni, 1933), 1:xi.

The Eliza Enigma: The Life and Legend of Eliza R. Snow

Maureen Ursenbach Beecher

> Using a topical approach, Maureen Ursenbach Beecher, editor at the Historical Department of The Church of Jesus Christ of Latter-day Saints, has dissected the career of Eliza R. Snow in order to consider the various facets of her active life. Dealing in turn with Eliza as poetess, prophetess, priestess, and presidentess, she finds much to interpret. Snow's poetry, for instance, was generally derivative. Like many New Englanders, Eliza anticipated a restoration of primitive Christianity, and like some other nineteenth-century Mormons, she seems to have had the insight confirmed by a personal revelation before joining the Church. Though she and other Church women operated under priesthood direction, the area of discretion for women within the Church seems to have been much greater in the mid-nineteenth century than today. Women conducted their own evangelical meetings and performed washings, anointings, and blessings to a much greater degree and with greater freedom than their late-twentieth-century sisters. Contrary to much of the mythology which has grown up around Eliza, however, Dr. Beecher finds Snow an expeditor and organizer rather than a creative originator. Snow seems to have taken others' ideas and put them into practice. By extension, the insights into the role of women in nineteenth-century Mormon society provided by this essay are enlightening and provocative.

"Poetess," "prophetess," "priestess," "presidentess," are terms which her contemporaries applied with reverent awe to Eliza Roxcy Snow. This woman, this "captain of Utah's woman host," commanded such respect among the Mormon women of Utah that they celebrated her birthday, whether or not she was among them. They took up a collection to pay her fare on a jaunt to the Holy Land. They turned out in numbers whenever and wherever she spoke on her many visits throughout the Great Basin kingdom. They listened to her, quoted her, obeyed her, and saw in her "the president of the female portion of the human race."[1] She was a legend before half her effective life was done, and lived that legend for the rest of it. She was aware of her position, and both played upon it and was plagued by it: "Sisters," she told an audience, "I occupy an honorable position, but the great responsibility attending it prevents my feeling proud."[2]

It is not difficult to catalog the public accomplishments of Eliza Snow. There is hardly an auxiliary organization in The Church of Jesus Christ of Latter-day Saints which does not bear her imprint: the women's Relief Society, which she helped found and then directed through its formative stages; Mormon Church youth groups, initiated with her support as Retrenchment Associations; and the children's Primary Association, carried by her from its birthplace in Farmington to nearly every settlement of the LDS Church in the West. And there are her published works: nine volumes extant, plus another tome of separately published pieces. Those are tangible reminders. Less obvious are the events now slid into history: the 1876 centennial territorial fair; the women's commission store; courses in medicine for women; the Deseret Hospital. And there is a long-enduring tradition of thought about women's place in church and society. Her contemporaries, and ours, have assessed her as a great woman. But then, as she saw it herself, "true greatness" is merely "usefulness."

What is elusive about Eliza--enigmatic, if you will--is the woman herself, the person within, the interior sources for the exterior strength. Or is it more appropriate, or accurate, to see her accomplishment in terms of the times and the needs of a band of Israel wandering their forty years--or was it forty months?--in the wilderness and then wresting from a desert Canaan their promised Zion? Whether the circumstances changed the woman or the woman altered the circumstances is a question to be left hanging while we dissect her life and the times into bits small enough for present scrutiny.

For that closer examination, let us take those four alliterative titles one by one: "poetess," "prophetess," "priestess," "presidentess." They are useful divisions of the areas of Eliza's activities; even more conveniently, they fit as chronological emphases in her life pattern. Each concern rises during its own period, reaches its zenith, and declines to a lesser but still significant level as the next rises. The cumulative effect is a piling up of interests and abilities,

characteristics of the one woman of Mormondom recognized by
the present Mormon laity and the historical community alike as
the epitome of Latter-day Saint womanhood. Questions, though,
arise in this generation's assessment of those qualities.
Therein lies the conflict of the life and the legend of Eliza
R. Snow.

Her life began in January 1804 in Becket, in the Berkshire
hills of Massachusetts, but she was soon transplanted to the
wild Ohio territory, then the Connecticut Western Reserve. The
Snows and their Ohio neighbors brought New England with them:
the same patriotic spirit which a generation earlier had inspired a revolution formed the attitudes of the Portage County
society in which Eliza grew. Her family was loyal American,
socially conscious (Oliver Snow was justice of the peace and
county commissioner in Mantua, Ohio), religious, educated
(Oliver Snow had taught school in Massachusetts and did again
for a term in Mantua), and intellectually liberal. They were
also practical, industrious, and financially successful. Eliza
grew from early childhood with a sense of family pride and a
reflected awareness of personal worth.[3]

School is easy for little girls with linguistic talents,
and Eliza had these in superfluous amounts. Bored with writing simple prose accounts of Mediterranean geography or the
battle of Hastings, she would compose her homework assignments
in verse, mimicking the patterns and themes of the poets she
read with insatiable appetite. It is not difficult to see her
as the pet of her teachers, and the sisters who followed seem
to have paled in comparison. None but her father seems to have
filled her need for intellectual companionship until Lorenzo,
her brother born when she was ten. Like his older sister, he
was often "shut up with his book." The two developed a close-
ness which lasted to her death.

But to return to the poetry: there seem to have been
examples enough for Eliza to follow in her own attempts at
versifying. Shakespeare and Milton were commonplace in the
United States by this time. The romantic poets had not yet
been discovered in America, but the styles and themes of the
eighteenth-century Rationalists were available, and that century's renewed interest in Greek and Roman classics had intro-
duced the literate to the ancient myths and the epic forms.
And every newspaper had its poetry column, filled with verses
of all varieties.

It was to the local newspaper that Eliza sent her first
public poem, an epic-styled celebration of the romantically
poignant "Battle of Missolonghi."

> Arise my infant muse, awake my lyre,
> To plaintive strains; but sing with cautious fear
> Lest thou profane, ...[4]

she wrote, choosing a poetic mode a cut above that of the usual poetry column offerings. Gaining confidence, she continued:

> Ye favor'd daughters, ye
> Who nurs'd on blest Columbia's happy soil
> Where the pure flag of liberty shall wave
> Till virtue's laurels wither on your breasts:

The lines scan well, in the formal iambic pentameter of Shakespeare. And the diction is as high flown as could be expected from a fledgling Milton. All told, this and the similarly high-toned elegiac ode on the deaths of Adams and Jefferson which followed in the same newspaper two weeks later demonstrate a literary sensitivity and a craftsmanship which augured well for a developing poet.[5] One would hope for the innovative, imaginative thrust to come to match the developing skill. A search through subsequent writings is disappointing. The two early odes, published in 1826 when Eliza was twenty-two, built in her a confidence which led, not to greater imagination, but to a popularizing of her style into form and subject matter more in keeping with what her contemporaries were submitting to the local papers:

> If there's a smile on nature's face
> It is the farmer's dwelling place

she writes in a homey poem called "The Farmer's Wife." The strict four-foot pattern, rhymed in unerring couplets, winds down to a simplistic conclusion:

> If you would make the best of life,
> Be, (if you can) the farmer's wife.[6]

One would like to imagine this as a sarcastic toying with both the genre and the society's simple mores--it would be about this time that Eliza received offers of marriage, probably from young men from neighboring farms. But, alas, the verses which follow leave us no recourse but to assume she had slipped easily, effortlessly, into the popular style of her times.

This is not to say the poetry is bad. On the contrary, some of it reads quite well, and the suggestion made in a later biographical sketch, that Eliza sacrificed a promising literary career to cast her lot with the Mormons, may not be far from wrong. Certainly the neighboring Cary sisters, Alice and Phoebe, wrote no better, and they, some twenty-five years behind Eliza, left their Ohio farm and moved to New York where they made an adequate living from their verses.

Eliza, however, had interests too diverse to devote her whole attention to poetry. Her life paced rapidly through the subsequent years from Mantua to Mormon Kirtland and on to Missouri in company with her adopted people. It was not until she found a period of relatively settled external circumstances, coupled with a disruptive emotional life, that the poetic gift reasserted itself with new promise. The place was Nauvoo, a seven-year stopover in the hegira of the Mormons, and the disruptive stimulus was the internal turmoil occasioned by her secret marriage to the prophet Joseph Smith, whom she later designated "the choice of my heart, the crown of my life."[7] That event proved the fulcrum on which her life balanced itself. Her diary entry for that day, 29 June 1842, reads: "This is a day of much interest to my feelings," and continues in a similar vein of ambiguous prose which ascends towards poetry as the emotion finds itself later "recalled in tranquility." Her next several poems in the diary all deal with her Joseph and her secret polygamous relationship with him.[8]

Among the usual verses, many of which found themselves, with or without her permission, in the Times and Seasons and the Millennial Star, are some confessional poems which approach the poetic standards from which present critics judge. In her retirement, "Where there's nobody here but Eliza and I," she could loose the reins, give her mind its soul, and compose such lines as these "Saturday Evening Thoughts":

> My heart is fix'd--I know in whom I trust.
> 'Twas not for wealth--'twas not to gather heaps
> Of perishable things--'twas not to twine
> Around my brow a transitory wreath,
> A garland deck'd with gems of mortal praise,
> That I foresook the home of childhood: that
> I left the lap of ease . . .[9]

In these times, though, she felt a responsibility beyond art and her own emotions. There were Saints to be cheered, and doctrines to be taught. "Zion's poetess," for so Joseph had named her, must turn her talents to the cause. The confessional writings extant from her Illinois period are far overshadowed numerically by such works as the poems to the gentile Quincy Whig pleading for aid and succor for the persecuted people; the hymns of encouragement to the distressed, that "though deep'ning trials throng [their] way," the Saints of God should "press on, press on"; and the doctrinally exciting "O My Father," written in this period as "Invocation, or the Eternal Father and Mother."

Eliza wrote on almost until her death, 1,200 miles and forty-one years from Nauvoo. Her collected poetry tells, better than many prose accounts, the history of a faith in the building, a nation in the making. In her verses can be found the whole sweep of the Mormon story. But as poetry, it fails of greatness. Twentieth-century critics find it superficial, maudlin, trite, and unimaginative.

As a poet, had she made no other contribution, Eliza might have been to us as obscure as Hannah Tapfield King is. But to her own contemporaries, Hannah King among them, she was muse, mentor, kindred in spirit. As that lady wrote to her:

> My Spirit bends instinctively to thine:
> At thy feet I fain would sit and learn
> Like Paul of old before Gamaliel.[10]

"Zion's poetess" to her literary disciples as to the rest of her Mormon contemporaries, she was building the reputation which would evolve into legend.

The poetic and the prophetic gifts are so closely related that one finds them hard to separate. Nor, perhaps, should one try. The title "prophetess" had a meaning to Eliza's nineteenth-century contemporaries which evades us now, in a church so regimented that the prophetic calling is by custom restricted not only to males in general, but to a specific body of Church leaders in particular. In a looser sense, however, one can see some prophetic functions beginning early in the life of Eliza R. Snow, growing as she finds and embraces the revelatory gospel, and reaching a peak of spirituality in that most unlikely of places, Winter Quarters, the Nebraska shanty town where the Mormons regrouped for their final push to Utah.

In search of her prophetic beginnings, let us backtrack to the first few years of Eliza's poetry publishing. In the 14 February 1829 issue of the Ravenna, Ohio, <u>Western Courier</u>, Eliza published a poem which in retrospect is a little disconcerting. It contains what could all too easily be interpreted as a prophecy of the Mormon restoration of the Christian gospel. The poem, dealing with the transience of life, contains these hope-infusing stanzas:

> But lo! a shining Seraph comes!
> Hark! 'tis the voice of sacred Truth;
> He smiles, and on his visage blooms,
> Eternal youth.

> He speaks of things before untold,
> Reveals what men nor angels knew,
> The secret pages now unfold
> To human view.

Years after her acceptance of the Mormon gospel, Eliza altered the phrase "secret pages" to read "long seal'd pages," to make more explicit the reference to the coming of the "Seraph," the angel Moroni, with the partially sealed plates from which the Book of Mormon was translated. Despite Eliza's later tamperings, we are left with the quandary: could she have heard, fully a year before its publication, of the book and its translator? Was she toying with a local rumor, carried, perhaps, by an itinerant preacher? Had she adopted the Campbellite hope of an angel coming to restore the true gospel? Or was there in her poetic imagination a kernel of true prophecy which prompted such a confident expression?

From the winter afternoon sometime in late 1830 or early 1831 when Joseph Smith warmed himself in her father's friendly living room, until her baptism into the new faith nearly five years later, Eliza struggled for direction. Her hesitation seems to have stemmed from a lack of spiritual confirmation. She yearned after the gifts of the spirit of which the New Testament spoke, and saw about her in the religions of the times, perhaps even somewhat in the new Mormon practices, either barren intellectualizing or, worse, sham perversions of the spiritual outpourings. Whatever led her to finally present herself for baptism at the hands of the Mormons, it was most surely not the fiery pentecostal assurance she wanted. But the night following her immersion into the waters of the new faith began her new visionary life. She received witness which she read as ultimate and divine confirmation:

> I had retired to bed, and as I was reflecting on the wonderful events transpiring around me, I felt an indescribable, tangible sensation . . . commencing at my head and enveloping my person and passing off at my feet, producing inexpressible happiness. Immediately following, I saw a beautiful candle with an unusual long, bright blaze directly over my feet. I sought to know the interpretation, and received the following, "The lamp of intelligence shall be lighted over your path." I was satisfied.[11]

The new faith led Eliza to Kirtland, where, despite the fact that she soon owned a house, she continued to live as governess in the home of the Prophet Joseph Smith. Her descriptions of the pentecostal manifestations accompanying the dedication of the temple there suggest a growing appetite for such outpourings as the speaking in tongues which became a regular part of temple worship--so much a part, in fact, that they had to be restricted to the last hour of the day-long Thursday fast meetings. We have no account of Eliza's participating in this prophesying and praising in tongues, but it is fair to assume that she was growing in her spiritual abilities, if only by intense observation.

From Kirtland, where Eliza was joined by her now converted parents, her sister Leonora, and her brother Lorenzo, the family moved to the newly founded community of Adam-ondi-Ahman in Missouri. The Snows traveled with, and settled near, the Huntington family, and undoubtedly in the move cemented the long-enduring friendship between Zina Diantha Huntington and Eliza R. Snow. Of Eliza's spiritual activity in the Missouri settlement there is no record, but we are told that Zina was practiced then in the gift of tongues,[12] and it is fair to assume that Eliza learned that communication, too. Until their deaths in Utah, Zina and Eliza practiced the prophetic speaking in and interpretation of tongues throughout the Church.

Expelled from Missouri, the two families and their core-ligionists moved to Illinois, aided in the building of Nauvoo, suffered the indignities of persecution, and in 1846 found themselves crossing Iowa. Privation and sickness create strife, even among the faithful, and Eliza details in her diary the bitterness which even she felt, she who had grown so emotionally strong and independent. Bickerings would have, could have, multiplied through the long winter of waiting for spring and the rest of the journey west. But there was something stronger than mutual privation to weld these people together, and Eliza was in the forefront of the practice. The women would gather in each other's tents for what might normally have been elite and cruelly cutting gossip sessions. But not so. Eliza records a series of gatherings:

> Spent the aft[er]n[oon] with Lucy in com[pany] of Zina, Loisa and Emily. E[mily] and myself spoke in the gift of tongues.[13]

And:

> Sis[ters] Sess[ions], Kim[ball], Whit[ney] and myself spent the eve[ning] at Sarah Ann's--had a pow'rful time--deep things were brought forth

And:
> which were not to be spoken.[14]

> . . . a time of blessing at sis[ter] K[imball]'s
> . . . . Sis[ter] Sess[ions] and myself blest
> Helen. I spoke and she interpreted. I then
> blest the girls in a song, singing to each in
> rotation.[15]

Such gatherings were not infrequent throughout the winter, and by spring Eliza seems to have emerged as the leader in the blessing meetings. Patty Sessions recorded on 1 May 1847:

> Sylvia and I went to a meeting to Sister Leonards.
> None but females there. We had a good meeting.
> I presided. It was got up by E. R. Snow. They
> spoke in toungues [sic]; I interpreted. Some
> prophesied. It was a feast.[16]

The gatherings, interrupted by the trek west, began again in the valley when Eliza would collect the women together in their rude homes in the Old Fort and the blessings and the prophesyings would again occur.

What was the nature of the prophecies and blessings uttered in the strange languages? Were they divinely inspired, or were they the emotional imaginings of a spiritually excited people? Who can know? In a retrospective tally of accounts we come up with what is most likely an unfair gauge: about half the recorded prophecies uttered by Eliza were fulfilled, about half were not. People to whom she promised the blessing of seeing the Savior return during their lifetime, or of standing in the temple to be built in Missouri, have died long since. But Heber J. Grant testified to his childhood memory of the prophecy uttered in tongues by Eliza, translated by Zina Huntington, that he would become an apostle. He did.[17] And Mary Ann Chadwick Hull, having buried two children in two years, was promised by Eliza that she would have a daughter (she was pregnant at the time) who would grow to womanhood.[18] The child, born healthy, was indeed a girl, and lived to age twenty. Two other daughters, one named after Eliza, outlived their mother.

But there are other prophetic gifts not so easily assessed. There are understandings and awarenesses which are a more important expression of prophecy than any number of predictions. Eliza is credited in Mormon thought with such insights. The favorite example is the concept of a Heavenly Mother, first expressed as doctrine in her "O My Father." General authorities have differed on the source of the revelation. Joseph F. Smith announced in 1895 that since God does not reveal his mind to a woman Eliza was taught the doctrine by Joseph Smith.[19] Wilford Woodruff, just two years earlier, remarked the singular appropriateness of the Lord's revealing such a profound doctrine through one of his daughters.[20] The historical evidence available seems, however inconclusively, to favor the former interpretation: Joseph Smith had comforted Zina Huntington, Eliza's friend and confidant, with the Mother-in-Heaven doctrine near the time of her own mother's death in 1839, six years before the poem was first published. Zina would doubtless have confided such revelation to her friend.

Other doctrines, less acceptable to modern Mormonism, worked themselves into Eliza's theology and found their way into her speeches and poems. One such was the theory which sent the ten tribes and the city of Enoch spinning off into outer space on detached particles of the earth. "Thou, Earth, wast once a glorious sphere," she wrote, consoling the globe for its loss.[21]

A study of the popular speculations of the times suggests that Eliza was seldom, if ever, the originator of the doctrines she accepted into her theology: Parley P. Pratt for one had expressed the spin-off idea as early as 1841; Eliza's poem is dated 1851. Eliza adopted ideas from whatever source she trusted--Joseph Smith's utterances would be received without question--and worked them meticulously into a neatly-packaged theology with the ends tucked in and the strings tied tight.

So it was, for example, when she published her composition reconciling the doctrine of literal resurrection of the body with the disconcerting evidences of decay and the cycles of nature. She followed Heber C. Kimball's suggested format: there are two parts to the body, one of which disintegrates and returns to earth, the other of which remains pure and untouched, awaiting the resurrection. She expressed the concept so well that her piece, first published in the Woman's Exponent in 1873, was reprinted in the Millennial Star in 1874 and again in the Exponent in 1875. At that time Brigham Young, prophet, president of the Church, and Eliza's husband, protested. A strict literalist, he was not for watering down scripture with such equivocating, and proclaimed so in a scathing editorial in the next issue of the Exponent. Six months later in a tiny box on a back page of the Deseret News appeared a carefully worded retraction written and signed by Eliza R. Snow.[22] A doctrine, especially someone else's doctrine, was hardly worth defying the priesthood over. Still, one wonders what conversation passed between the two of them in the intervening six months as they met each evening in the family prayer service in the Beehive House.

But do such lapses indicate the absence of prophetic gifts? The testimony of her contemporaries would refute such denial. From St. George to Cache Valley they witnessed to her perceptive preaching, her vast knowledge, and her speaking in tongues--"Eve's tongue," as she termed the Adamic language--in their meetings, where she uttered blessings they were sure were prophetic. Men and women alike attested to her spiritual calling. We are again left with the enigma: Did her gifts include that of prophecy? Was she a prophetess in the present sense of the word? The life and the legend are a hundred years away from us.

Because of her involvement in the practice of the Mormon temple endowment, Eliza R. Snow was called "High Priestess." As early as Nauvoo, where she was recorder in the temple, and later in the Salt Lake Endowment House, where she presided over the women's section, she performed the holy ordinances for the faithful of her sex, often blessing them with a special blessing beyond the scope of the ceremonies themselves. Her equivalent in a modern LDS temple would be the matron, who is by tradition the wife of the temple president.

It is understandable that Eliza's image would take on a special holiness in the eyes of the women of the Church, that the aura of sacred mystery which covers the secret ordinances of the temple should somehow cling to her. It did indeed become a part of the legend, an addition to the atmosphere which surrounded her in the eyes of her contemporaries. Added to the gifts of the spirit which she was practicing, the temple calling was the official sanction, the title, which justified the reverence which they would accord her.

Other functions she performed, now generally restricted to priesthood holders, were likewise in keeping with the title _priestess_. Blessing the sick, administering to those who requested it, and washing and anointing women about to be confined were frequent with her. Eliza was not the only woman to whom the sisters would appeal for these ministrations; often a community or group would have among its number some sister who seemed especially gifted for the purpose. But it was Eliza whose word gave the practice official sanction, who taught the proper forms, and who specified the qualifications of sisters who might minister.

That the practice was linked to Eliza's name is clear from a letter, dated 1901, in which a sister is questioning the quasi-official suggestion that the women no longer administer to the sick. "Eliza R. Snow taught us how to do it," is the sense of the letter. "Should we not continue to follow her directions?"[23] An official statement is recorded in two circular letters, one of indeterminate date on stationery of the Relief Society, the other dated 3 October 1914 over the signatures of the First Presidency with Joseph F. Smith as President. Their intent is the same: women may indeed administer with consecrated oil, "confirming" rather than "sealing" the blessing, making no mention of authority. They may also continue the practice of washing and anointing women about to give birth.²⁴ In other words, the practice promoted by Eliza Snow, following the approval of Joseph Smith, continued well into this century, and perpetuated the name of Eliza R. Snow as priestess to the women of the Church.

By 1855, or thereabouts, when Brigham Young called Eliza to facilitate the reorganizing of the Relief Societies in some of the Salt Lake Stake wards, the women over whom she would preside had already defined her in the roles to which we have paid note. Already "poetess," "prophetess," and "priestess," she could well expect to bring to the function of "presidentess" the admiration and respect of the women, irrespective of whatever administrative skills she might possess.

Fortunately for Brigham Young and for the Church, she did have the ability to preside. As clerk to her father, who had been a public administrator during her Ohio youth, she would have learned something of matters of government. Later, when some Nauvoo women had decided in Sarah Kimball's sitting room to organize a women's benevolent society and needed a constitution, it was to Eliza they turned, evidence that her understanding of such matters was early recognized.

The Nauvoo Female Relief Society, organized not according to the constitution Eliza drew up, but rather under the priesthood direction of Joseph Smith, elected Eliza its secretary. Her minutes indicated a lively interest in the processes of government, and by the time Brigham Young had need of her abilities, she had learned about leadership. By 1867, when the ward Relief Societies in Utah demonstrated the need for an auxiliary direction, she was the logical head of the first general board. Her sense of stewardship led her throughout the existing Church, organizing groups where there had been none, and strengthening and directing existing societies. Her message was always, "We will do as we are directed by the Priesthood";²⁵ but when a priesthood leader seemed about to thwart one of the Relief Society projects, her response was that he should be "reasoned" with. She was confident of her programs and of her and her sisters' ability to facilitate them.

Eliza R. Snow--"Sister Snow" to him--was a plural wife of Brigham Young, their marriage having taken place in Nauvoo in early 1846. Far from the adoration with which she honored Joseph was the respect with which she followed Brigham. "Followed," I am persuaded, is the right word, for as independent as she seems in her activities in behalf of the women of the Church, she restricted her jurisdiction to the stewardship

assigned her by Brigham. This was not as constraining as it
sounds: she and "President Young," as she always called him,
saw eye to eye on most things. Exceptions are the incident
of the paper on resurrection and one homey little story about
her having hidden away one of his daughter's silk sashes,
deeming it inappropriate to the President's daughter in those
times of needed retrenchment. Brigham made her give it back,
but later, with Eliza's help, established the Retrenchment
Society, with goals similar to Eliza's purpose in taking away
the sash in the first place. These two, Eliza and Brigham,
thought and worked together; only slight misunderstanding required discussion. Confirmation by each of the other's projects was almost pro forma. More a counselor than a wife,
Eliza seems to have carried as much authority as Brigham
Young's counselors in the Presidency, at least in regard to
women's activities.

In administering the affairs of the women (which included,
as she defined them, responsibilities towards the children and
young ladies--hence her involvement with Primary and Retrenchment associations) Eliza seems to have been a paragon of administrative skill and a dynamo of executive energy. She lacked
but one quality, that same quality which inhibited her poetry
and limited her doctrinal insight: she had little imagination,
little creative spark. She was not an innovator. The story
repeats itself in the history of every project with which her
name is initially associated. It was Sarah Kimball, not
Eliza, who sparked the founding of Relief Society in Salt Lake
City, as she had in Nauvoo; it was when Louisa Greene came to
Eliza with the proposal for a magazine that the Woman's
Exponent was founded; and it was Aurelia Rogers who first expressed her idea of a Primary Association to Eliza. In each
case Eliza was not the originator, but an initial executor of
the project; not the agent, but the catalyst. Once she adopted
a suggestion, however, Eliza changed roles. Codifying the
concept into an organizational format, she would travel from
one end of the Mormon settlement to the other implementing it.
In one remarkable jaunt to southern Utah in 1880-81, the
seventy-six-year-old woman rode nearly two thousand miles by
train and wagon to establish some thirty-five Primaries among
the Saints there.

In one concern of high importance to the women of Utah,
however, she was less than a leader. Supportive, yes, but
only peripherally so. That was the movement for women's
rights, as active then as it is now. Most of the time and on
some of the issues the Church was officially on the side of
the crusading women. Suffrage for women had the official blessing of Church leaders. Utah early gave the franchise to women,
and Eliza's name headed the list of those who addressed to

41

acting governor Stephen Mann their thanks for signing the bill
into law. But the following year, aside from encouraging the
women to vote, she predicted their passivity in the political
arena:

> Although invested with the right of suffrage,
> [she told a group in Ogden] we shall never
> have occasion to vote for lady legislators or
> for lady congressmen.[26]

One might wish we had reason in our time to trust her optimistic belief that

> the kingdom of God, of which we are citizens,
> will never be deficient in a supply of good
> and wise men to fill governmental positions,
> and of brave men for warriors.[27]

With all the other responsibilities she carried, Eliza
surely cannot be faulted for not adding the women's rights
movement to her leadership load. The question is, however,
less one of activity than one of doctrine.[28] She firmly believed that a woman's divinely appointed role bound her kindly
but firmly to the home. The building of the kingdom, she admitted, required that some mothers make the sacrifice of leaving home to obtain medical training, or to be the telegraphers,
sales clerks, bookkeepers, and typesetters that President Young
needed. The woman's sphere, she affirmed with some justification, was nowhere so wide as in Utah among the Mormons, especially guaranteeing as Mormons did the most important right of
women: the right of wedlock. Plural marriage, polygyny, was
her answer to the feminists who pled the cause of women in
Utah.

The logic may seem elusive, but typically for Eliza, it
could all be made to fit. Justifying the status quo, the subjection in which most women found themselves vis-à-vis their
male counterparts, she referred to the parents of the human
race and the original sin. Eve was the first to partake of the
fruit, and so deserved her punishment:

> She led in the transgression, and was plac'd
> By Eloheim's unchangeable decree
> In a subservient and a dependent sphere.[29]

And almost as though "whatever is, is right," Eliza accepted
that judgment and built around it--with some doctrinal suggestions from such men as Orson Hyde and George Q. Cannon--a theology which she could make consistent with the rest of her

beliefs. Where there is organization, she insisted, there
must be gradation. Eve having been the first to sin, her
daughters were placed in the secondary position. God ordained
it, and Eliza would not protest. She affirmed:

> We stand in a different position from the la-
> dies of the world; we have made a covenant with
> God, we understand his order, and know that
> order requires submission on the part of woman.[30]

But the "curse of Eve"--that her desire should be to her husband and that he should rule over her--was not to last forever.
As Adam had found redemption from his sins, so also would Eve
from hers. In that same 1871 discourse cited above she explained how the curse would be lifted:

> The Lord has placed the means in our hands, in
> the Gospel, whereby we can regain our lost posi-
> tion. But how? Can it be done by rising, as
> women are doing in the world, to clamor for our
> rights? No. . . . It was through disobedience
> that woman came into her present position, and
> it is only by honoring God in all the institu-
> tions he has revealed to us, that we can come
> out from under that curse, regain the position
> originally occupied by Eve, and attain to a ful-
> ness of exaltation in the presence of God.[31]

The "institution" through which a woman could honor God and
regain her lost equality with man was, ironically, plural
marriage. Eve disobeyed, she reasoned; her daughters must
obey--but in righteousness. Righteous men are less numerous
than deserving women: hence, polygyny. The inconsistent
intervening steps in the syllogism seem not to have disturbed
Eliza in her reasoning. Her pattern allowed for so many goods:
order, the growth of the kingdom through large families, equality among women (theoretically, at least), and peace with the
brethren. The day when women would receive "the power of
reigning and the right to reign"[32] was far off in reality, but
near enough to put a rosy cast over the whole question and to
justify the status quo, in which she found herself and her
sisters, she assumed, to be quite fulfilled. Eliza, then, was
not a feminist in the Elizabeth Cady Stanton mold any more
than in the Gloria Steinem pattern. First things must come
first, and in Eliza's view many concerns came before "women's
rights" as the society at large interpreted them.

So in all her presiding she failed to lead out in what
seems to some women today to have been the major issue; and in

her definition of "What Is and What Is Not for Woman" she sold short her sex, by today's lights. So in much of her poetry she let ease and usefulness and dedication to her cause outweigh the finer poetic crafts. So some of her prophecies were inspired more by millennial enthusiasm than by divine witness. So her priestly functions have all but disappeared from Mormon practice. Those are only parts of the whole, a whole which, when we draw back far enough to see Eliza in the broader social landscape, takes on an aspect larger than the sum of its parts.

For there is no equivocating over the position she held, or the influence she wielded over the Mormon women of her time. The five thousands who filled the tabernacle to hear her defense of polygamy, or the one whom she warmly embraced for her faithfulness to her calling--all these attested, on whatever grounds, to her leadership.

If she was not the potter whose firm hand shaped the infant faith of the new society, Eliza was certainly the kilnsman who fired the newly-molded piece into a hard and solid form. And if the edges are chipping away under the pressures of this century's demands, that form still stands recognizably as she left it.

REFERENCES

The author acknowledges the invaluable assistance of Jill Mulvay and others of the Historical Department of The Church of Jesus Christ of Latter-day Saints, and the encouragement and support of Leonard J. Arrington, Church Historian and Director of the Charles Redd Center for Western Studies.

1. Woman's Exponent, 9(1 April 1881):165.

2. Ibid., 4(15 August 1875):42.

3. Orrin Harmon, "Historical Facts Appertaining to the Township of Mantua . . . , Portage Co. Ohio," handwritten manuscript, 1866, in the Western Reserve Historical Society, Cleveland, Ohio; see also History of Portage County, Ohio (Chicago, 1885), pp. 475-85, the chapter dealing with Mantua Township.

4. Western Courier (Ravenna, Ohio), 22 July 1826; see also Week-day Religious Education, 1(March 1937):6-7.

5. Western Courier, 5 August 1826.

6. Eliza R. Snow, Diary and Notebook, photocopy of holograph, Church Archives, Historical Department, The Church of Jesus Christ of Latter-day Saints, Salt Lake City, Utah, hereinafter cited as LDS Church Archives.

7. Woman's Exponent, 15(1 August 1886):37.

8. Eliza R. Snow, Diary and Notebook, 29 June 1842 ff.

9. Ibid., 16 November 1842; see also Eliza R. Snow, Poems, Religious, Historical, and Political, 2 vols. (Liverpool, 1856; and Salt Lake City, 1877), 1:3-6.

10. Hannah Tapfield King, "Lines, Affectionately Addressed to Sister Eliza Snow," photocopy of manuscript, LDS Church Archives.

11. Eliza R. Snow, An Immortal: Selected Writings of Eliza R. Snow (Salt Lake City, Utah, 1957), p. 6.

12. Benjamin F. Johnson, "'Aunt Zina' as I have Known Her from Youth," handwritten manuscript, Zina Card Brown Collection, LDS Church Archives.

13. Eliza R. Snow, Diary, 1 June 1846 to 16 August 1849, under date 2 June 1847, microfilm of holograph, LDS Church Archives.

14. Ibid., 3 June 1847.

15. Ibid., 6 June 1847.

16. Patty Sessions, Diary, 1 May 1847, holograph, LDS Church Archives.

17. Heber J. Grant in Conference Report of The Church of Jesus Christ of Latter-day Saints, April 1927, pp. 17-18.

18. "Sketch of the Life of Mary Ann Chadwick Hull," Library of Congress Diaries, microfilm of typescript, p. 4, LDS Church Archives.

19. Joseph F. Smith, "Discourse," Deseret Evening News, 9 February 1895; discourse delivered 20 January 1895.

20. Wilford Woodruff, "Discourse," The Latter-day Saints' Millennial Star, 56(9 April 1894):229; discourse delivered 8 October 1893.

21. Eliza R. Snow, "Address to Earth," Poems, 1:153. The verse was first published in the Deseret News, 31 May 1851.

22. Woman's Exponent 2(1 December 1873):99, and 4(1 September 1875):54. Brigham Young's reprimand follows in 4(15 September 1875):60; Eliza's retraction is in Deseret News Weekly, 5 April 1876.

23. Louisa Lula Greene Richards to Lorenzo Snow, 9 April 1901, LDS Church Archives.

24. James R. Clark, ed., Messages of the First Presidency, 5 vols. (Salt Lake City, 1970), 4:312-17.

25. Eliza R. Snow to [Willmirth] East, 23 April 1883, Eliza R. Snow Papers, LDS Church Archives.

26. Deseret News, 26 July 1871.

27. Ibid.

28. Eliza Snow's stand on the whole question of woman's rights is discussed more fully in Jill Mulvay's "Eliza R. Snow and the Woman Question," manuscript in the files of the LDS Church Historian.

29. Eliza R. Snow, "The New Year, 1852," Deseret News, 10 January 1852.

30. "Miss E. R. Snow's Address to the Female Relief Societies of Weber County," Latter-day Saints' Millennial Star, 33(12 September 1871):578.

31. Ibid.

32. Eliza R. Snow, "Woman," Poems, 2:178.

McCarthyism in the Mountains, 1950-1954
F. Ross Peterson

In recent years, it seems, politics in the United States has swung away from conditions which existed in the early 1950s. McCarthyism as a political tactic has been discredited and organizations like the FBI and CIA which allowed themselves and their agents to be used for political purposes by right wing forces are currently under attack for allegedly illegal activities. Clearly, a great deal has changed in two decades.

In this essay, however, F. Ross Peterson of Utah State University, author of a biography of Senator Glen Taylor, has gone back to the earlier era. Though McCarthyism as a tactic is shown to have been only marginally effective, the long list of politicians who used the tactic or allowed it to be used in their behalf includes such congressmen and senators as Wallace F. Bennett of Utah, Henry Dworshak of Idaho, and William Henry Harrison of Wyoming. The tactic consisted of the use of lies, half-truths, and innuendo spread by various publications, by fellow politicians, and by professional anti-Communists and former FBI agents. During this period political discourse in the United States reached what was perhaps its nadir, and it may be poetic justice that the tide should have turned against those like Richard Nixon who formerly used these methods to unfairly smear their opponents with charges of Communist sympathy and disloyalty to the United States.

In December 1954, by a vote of sixty-seven to twenty-two, Senator Joseph R. McCarthy was censured by the United States Senate. For nearly five years every decision made by a United States President had to be weighed as to how it would affect Joseph McCarthy and his followers. He left his name,

"McCarthyism," as a haunting reminder of an unpleasant episode in America's recent past. Few geographical regions were affected as directly as the Mountain West.[1]

In setting the stage for a discussion of McCarthyism in the mountain states, a brief description of post-World War II America is warranted. The political climate of 1945-50 was shaped by a new and frightening phenomenon, the Cold War; by the agitation of conservative special interest groups; and by the disintegration of New Deal-type liberalism.[2] However, politicians still had to mobilize the support necessary for a politics of anti-Communism. There were many Republican and Democratic conservatives who championed the anti-Communism issues and maintained that Rooseveltian liberalism was leading the nation down a winding path that could only lead to Communism.

Once these domestic critics realized there were internal security issues created by the Cold War, they had more ammunition against the Democratic administrations. Conservatives charged that the Roosevelt and Truman presidencies were tolerant of disloyalty and subversion at home and were "soft on Communism" in Europe and Asia. Consequently, a long series of congressional investigations was launched, designed not only to locate subversives but also to embarrass the federal government.[3]

By 1948 Harry Truman's administration had responded to the investigations and charges in a unique way. The foreign policy of containment was defended with firm anti-Communist rhetoric. A federal loyalty-security program was instituted and U.S. Communist Party leaders were prosecuted. Truman even went so far as to use the Communist issue against the Progressive Party in the 1948 campaign. Once committed to this course of action, Truman hoped to silence his critics, but he failed. By 1950, conservatives denounced Truman for the loss of China and for the Korean War and demanded a purge within the government.[4] Even the passage of the McCarran Internal Security Act failed to appease a suspicious and fearful populace.

Political leaders, including Harry Truman, succeeded in creating a mood conducive to demagoguery. Joseph McCarthy's charges and attacks on American policy resonated through the system because they were typical, not because they were new and unique. This political impulse came to be called "McCarthyism" because of the specificity and daring of his accusations. It should be remembered that McCarthy was the product of anti-Communist politics; he was not its progenitor. In all probability, even if McCarthy had never made those February 1950 speeches in Wheeling, West Virginia, and in Salt Lake City, what America came to call "McCarthyism" would nevertheless have characterized American national politics at mid-century.[5]

An examination of McCarthyism as a political technique in the Mountain West is most applicable if the above is kept in mind. Joseph McCarthy's direct impact on elections in the four states under study was minimal; yet the methods he perfected played a significant role. Those techniques and tactics are simplified to mean campaign accusations claiming that a political opponent has had Communist associations or is idealogically compatible with the Communists.

It is also essential to realize that the Communist issue was a national concern and did not originate with the various candidates at the local level. For this reason, as well as others, it is necessary to focus on six United States senatorial campaigns in the four states. In part because McCarthy was a senator, it seems that senatorial campaigns offer the best case studies of McCarthyism in action.

Both Idaho and Utah had senatorial elections in 1950, the year McCarthyism invaded mountain states politics. Since the Idaho race was a heated primary battle, it will be discussed first. No Democratic incumbent senator was more vulnerable than Idaho's Glen H. Taylor. A former vaudeville actor and country western singer, Taylor had been branded a Communist sympathizer by opponents in both parties ever since he entered Idaho politics in 1938. After finally gaining a Senate seat in 1944, Taylor went to Washington and established a consistent liberal record. However, Taylor became disturbed over the Cold War and believed the United States was in part responsible, so he left the Democratic party in 1948 and ran for Vice-President on Henry Wallace's Progressive Party ticket. The Wallace effort was tainted as "red" from its inception and Taylor's participation left him wide open to attacks when he sought re-election in 1950.[6]

Glen Taylor knew that he was going to be smeared by the political opposition, in part because Taylor had spoken out against McCarthy's "Red Scare" from the beginning. Just eighteen days after McCarthy's notorious speech in Wheeling, West Virginia, Taylor criticized McCarthy on the Senate floor and inserted in the Congressional Record an editorial which attacked the Wisconsin senator's first assertion, that the federal government was filled with Communists.[7] In a Boise radio speech during the 1950 campaign, Taylor referred to Truman's offer to open State Department files to the Senate committee investigating McCarthy's charges, saying, "McCarthy is not satisfied with that--he wants the FBI files, too. I am convinced, however, that if he got the FBI files, he wouldn't be satisfied but would probably insist on seeing the books of St. Peter in a last desperate effort to prevent final collapse of this whole fantastic business." It was Taylor's expressed hope that the public would "rise up and demand an end to it all." He declared, "It is difficult to decide whether free institutions are more in danger from the activities of the secret police or from the activities of subversive characters."[8]

Try as he would, Taylor was unable to make political headway by pointing to the dangers of extremist actions. Both Democrats and Republicans viciously attacked the Idaho senator for his alleged Communist leanings. The invasion of South Korea by the North Koreans in June 1950 gave considerable aid to the anti-Taylor forces despite the fact that Taylor supported the attempt to halt North Korea because it was a United Nations action.[9]

D. Worth Clark, Taylor's principal primary opponent, said that the Korean situation emphasized the need for "elimination of our Henry Wallaces from positions of power in public life. A public official doesn't have to be a card-carrying communist to be a communist stooge or dupe."[10] Repeatedly Clark accused Taylor of being "duped by communists into playing their game at the expense of Americanism."[11] Clark, who had served in the China lobby after his term in the Senate, criticized Taylor for refusing to vote for aid to China prior to the Communist takeover in 1949. He claimed that American boys were now being killed in Korea because of "Taylor and his Communist associates."[12]

Compared to the Republican attacks on Taylor, however, Clark's charges were mild. The Idaho GOP picked up Senator McCarthy's theme and applied it to the Democratic incumbent.[13] The most vociferous Republican was Payette attorney Herman Welker, who was seeking the Republican senatorial nomination. Although Welker faced two other Republicans in the contest for the Senate nomination, he ignored his GOP opposition and concentrated his entire fire on Taylor. In a speech on July 4, Welker announced that there were "87 communists in Idaho," plus many more "radicals and stooges and crackpots who consistently follow the party line and play right into the hands of the communist cause. I include the Henry Wallaces and Glen Taylors."[14]

Welker repeatedly challenged Taylor to a debate, but the incumbent steadfastly refused to discuss anything with Welker. Taylor took the position that he was running against Clark and White in the primary, and therefore he tried to ignore Welker and his barrage of charges. John McMurray, Welker's campaign manager, claimed that Taylor was dodging Welker because the Payette lawyer "would rip Taylor and his communist-line activities into shreds and Taylor knows it."[15] In a Lewiston speech, Welker attacked Taylor because the senator refused to "debate his Americanism with me," and added that Taylor's friendship "with the communists" was a great source of embarrassment for Idaho.[16] Welker categorized Taylor as a "political coward who hasn't the courage to debate me. He knows I would hang his hide on the fence . . . and expose his communist-line activities."[17]

One of Taylor's supporters, John Carver, did agree to debate Welker concerning Taylor's record. After listening to Welker's familiar spiel, Carver calmly told a Caldwell audience that if the public "analyzed the charges, they have no substance." According to Carver, it took "courage to run for the vice-presidency on the third party ticket, and then courage to come back in the Democratic party." Carver logically asserted that "if communists supported the third party, that doesn't mean the third party is Communist. . . . This campaign of smear is achieving a new low."[18]

Clark, Welker, and the other senatorial candidates of both parties were indebted to the Idaho Daily Statesman for much of the material used in their attacks on Taylor. The Boise daily, long one of Taylor's severest critics, launched an unparalleled assault on Taylor and his record. According to John Corlett, the political editor, it was the only time that he ever set out, "under the direction of my publisher and editor, to destroy a person and that person's philosophy."[19]

In the July 2 editorial entitled "A Man Is Judged by the Company He Keeps . . . and by What He Does," the Statesman declared war on Taylor. The paper stated that it intended to run a series patterned after the pamphlet used against Claude Pepper in Florida, "The Red Record of Claude Pepper." It also set the tone for its subsequent attacks on Taylor by quoting Paul Robeson, the black singer and Soviet sympathizer who had said, "The Soviet Union is the only country I've been in where I felt completely at ease." The paper then asserted that Robeson was an "acquaintance" of Taylor's and claimed that Robeson had been identified with the Communist party since 1936. In conclusion the Statesman used a quotation from the Daily Worker, which called Taylor and Pepper "the heroes of the 80th Congress."[20]

Day after day throughout early July, the Boise daily published sections of "The Red Record of Claude Pepper," which had been prepared by a former FBI agent, Lloyd C. Leemis. At the same time, the paper devoted a considerable amount of editorial space to scathing assaults on Taylor for "consorting with known Communists." After establishing what the paper considered a direct correlation between Taylor, Pepper, and the Communists, the Statesman abruptly shifted its attack to Taylor alone, with the publication of a series called "The Red Record of Glen Taylor--As He Made It."[21]

In the initial editorial of this series, Taylor was accused of participating in so-called Communist-front groups such as the Congress of Civil Rights, the Win-the-Peace Conference, and the National Council of American-Soviet Friendship, all included in the attorney general's catalog of subversive organizations. Quoting from Taylor's speeches in opposition to the Truman Doctrine, the Marshall Plan, NATO, and the Universal Military Training Act, the paper compared the positions he had taken with those of the <u>Daily Worker</u> or some official of the Soviet Union. Contending that Taylor did not represent Idaho or America, the paper accused the senator of "representing the Russians on the floor of the United States Senate with more words than all the other senators in history."[22]

It is difficult to assess the effect of the Boise newspaper's campaign, but on July 28 three prominent Idaho Democrats called Taylor a Communist or placed him squarely in the Communist camp.[23] When Taylor repeatedly accused his opponents of trying to smear him and his record, the <u>Statesman</u> replied with a quotation from J. Edgar Hoover, director of the FBI, who had warned that "crying smear" was part of the Communist line. The newspaper maintained that "the 'smear' accusation is a smokescreen which more and more Idahoans are understanding every day."[24] When Taylor criticized the paper's drive to unseat him, the Boise daily retorted, "It's the Communist line because the Communists fear the free press."

All Taylor's words opposing American foreign policy were labeled as "imbedded in Communist favor."[25] There was no mention of Taylor's genuine concern over the possibility of a third World War. His liberal stand for the civil rights of all Americans, whether they were blacks, laborers, or Communists, was not mentioned; nor were respected Americans who agreed with Taylor. The paper ignored the fact that many Idahoans, including Corlett, the paper's political editor, had expressed the belief that Taylor was doing a good job of representing Idaho's specific interests in the Senate.[26] In short, the <u>Statesman's</u> attack on Taylor was a sad example of the rampant extremism and hysteria that was becoming a national trend.

After attempting to emphasize what he considered to be the issues, Taylor finally accepted the Boise daily's offer of a full page in which to reply to the paper's charges. He added the condition that his material must be printed exactly as submitted. Margaret Cobb Ailshie, the publisher, wanted Taylor to confine himself to Communism, but doubted that "a single newspaper page will be sufficient." Following a few days of bickering about censorship, Taylor bought a full-page ad in the <u>Statesman</u> instead of accepting Mrs. Ailshie's offer so that he could put in it what he wanted.[27]

Among the items Taylor placed on the page he had purchased was a photograph that had appeared previously in the <u>Statesman</u> and the <u>Idaho Falls Post Register</u>. It was a picture taken in

Washington, showing the Idaho congressional delegation greeting Wilson Chandler, president of Idaho's Junior Chamber of Commerce. In the Statesman's version, Taylor had been cut out of the picture entirely, leaving the impression that the Democratic senator was not present, which, according to Taylor, was "a deliberate lie." On the same page, Taylor also reproduced an article from the Statesman which carried the subheading "Favors Socialized Medicine." The first sentence of the article, however, was a quotation from a speech in which Taylor denied that he was a proponent of "socialized medicine."[28] The headline, Taylor claimed, was obviously a manipulation of the truth.

The third item on the purchased page was an open letter to Mrs. Ailshie, in which Taylor wrote, "Communism is not the issue. . . . I am no Communist, and you know it. Otherwise, you would not have been so careful to avoid making the direct charge." The Idaho senator told Mrs. Ailshie, "Doubtless you would relish the spectacle if I would get down and wallow in the mire with your paid character assassins, but I long ago learned a lesson." Referring to the pictures reproduced on the page, he asserted: "If a newspaper will indulge in the deliberate misrepresentation and deceit in its day-to-day reporting of the news so graphically demonstrated on this page, it would hardly seem necessary to rehash a series of charges so obviously designed to distort and misrepresent."[29]

Taylor's rebuttal had some logic, but lacked the impact of a month of "The Red Record." The fact is that it was too feeble to counteract the vicious attacks of the Statesman. Instead of denying the substance of the paper's charges, he had attacked the techniques employed by the newspaper.

Glen Taylor was defeated by less than 1,000 votes in the 1950 primary. The most important factor in bringing about his defeat was his alleged Communism.[30] Another factor was that the Republican party encouraged its members to cross over and vote for Clark in the open Democratic primary. John Corlett estimated that between 3,000 and 5,000 did just that. As early as May 28, the Statesman had openly advised Idaho Republicans to "organize, support Clark and defeat both Taylor and White in the primaries."[31] Shortly before the election, Ray McKaig, a longtime Taylor enemy, similarly advised his fellow Republicans, adding that "America will not survive with men like Alger Hiss and Glen Taylor leading America into Communism."[32]

Although an editorial in the Lewiston Morning Tribune of 11 August 1950 predicted that Taylor was not finished politically, for all intents and purposes he was.[33] Taylor's opposition to the measures designed to curb Communist aggression abroad and to ferret out disloyal subjects in the United States meant that he was once again out of step with the crowd.

Persistent as ever, Taylor sought a Senate seat in 1954, but he found that the "Red Scare" was still very much in evidence, as it was in Utah in 1950.

In some ways, Senator Elbert Thomas, the veteran three-term New Dealer from Utah, was similar to Glen Taylor. Thomas, a political science professor, had unseated Reed Smoot in the Roosevelt landslide of 1932 and then defended his office against the president of Brigham Young University, Franklin S. Harris, and another LDS leader, Adam S. Bennion.[34] An active, devout Mormon, Thomas was victimized in 1950 as much from outside the state as from within.

Early in the election year, the Utah Republicans decided to concentrate on the senatorial race and to attack Thomas in three areas--his age, his record, and his alleged association with Communism. They nominated Wallace F. Bennett, the former president of the conservative National Association of Manufacturers. Although there were other issues, this discussion will center on the McCarthyistic techniques employed against Elbert Thomas.

Like many other liberals, Thomas had permitted his name to be used during the 1940s as a sponsor of certain organizations later pronounced as subversive by the United States' Attorney General. A scholar, Thomas had published a book, The Four Fears, as well as an article in a leftist journal, The New Masses. Thomas's writing always espoused liberalism as the answer to America's future. Unlike Taylor, Thomas was not assailed from his own party. Indeed, the most devastating assaults came from Chicago, St. Louis, and Minneapolis, not Utah.

Jeremiah Stokes, a former Utahn who resided in Chicago, researched Thomas for nearly a decade. His conclusions were published in a thirty-nine-page pamphlet which Stokes delivered to prominent Utah Republicans, including Governor J. Bracken Lee. Stokes tried to document Thomas's alleged connections with Communists, fellow-travelers, and Communist-front organizations. All that Stokes really proved was that Thomas had been listed as a co-sponsor of some pro-Soviet groups and that the Daily Worker had praised Thomas for some votes and statements.

Stokes's pamphlet was followed by another key propaganda item which hit Utah a few weeks before the election. A black and white mass-produced paper sheet filled with fantastic accusations circulated throughout Utah. It boldly headlined that "Senator Elbert Thomas Presides at Communist Meeting" and described how Thomas, sympathetic to Communism, presided at a New Masses fund raising dinner. Thomas was pictured next to Paul Robeson, who was described by the broadside as "one of the most dangerous Communists in America." Numerous other sponsors were listed between the two pictures and were described as

"Communists and their sympathizers."36
    At the bottom of the page was a list of questions directed toward Senator Thomas. It included such interrogatories as "Why did you preside at the Communist banquet? If you knew it was a Communist banquet why did you accept? Why do you not apologize to the citizens of Utah and America for presiding at a Communist money-raising campaign dinner?"37 The circular was prepared by the American Anti-Communist League in St. Louis and distributed to Utahns by the Utah Anti-Communist League, which was Marilyn R. Allen.38

    The irony of the "Presides at Communist Meeting" paper was that Thomas did not even attend the meeting. Paul Robeson was not at the banquet either. But as the circular was distributed in undetermined numbers throughout the state, the truth was a difficult commodity to peddle. Both the Democrats and Thomas replied indignantly against the broadside. Thomas called it the "most false, defamatory, insidious, dishonest, and hateful attack upon a man's good name and character that I have ever seen."

    The Republicans simply countered with yet another bombshell of significant power to retire Elbert Thomas permanently. Walter E. Quigley, a Minnesota extremist, had dedicated himself to anti-Communism and to thwarting those politicians he thought were supporting the Communist movement. Late in October, Quigley published a four-page issue of the United States Senate News. It was a newspaper-sized spread of Thomas's alleged Communist record and was sent to every telephone subscriber in the state of Utah. It was also left in piles to be picked up by passersby in the Salt Lake City area. The newspaper showed Thomas's connection with many of the same questionable organizations and persons mentioned in the Stokes and Allen literature. It gave rise to the inference that each such association of Thomas was intended to promote the Communist cause.39

    Quigley's Senate News contained seven cartoons that portrayed Thomas as a puppet of labor unions, a dupe of Communists, a proponent of socialized medicine, and an opponent of military preparedness. Also included were a number of blaring headlines that amplified the themes of the cartoons. The formula Quigley utilized was quite simple. The Daily Worker was Communist; Senator Thomas's name and picture appeared in the Daily Worker; therefore, Senator Thomas was a Communist. This formula was designed to create guilt by association and was repeated throughout the paper.40

    One story was designed to protect Quigley's paper from a counterattack by warning the readers that it would be attacked. "The present administration will, immediately on publication of this paper turn loose a barrage of propaganda to discredit it. They will scream that the people from outside the state are attempting to interfere in Utah politics."41 Consequently,

Quigley disarmed the Democrats and Thomas before they could
reply to the guilt by association charges. The paper confi-
dently stated, "Every item in this paper is documented either
by photostatic evidence or by specific reference to an official
government document."[42] Quigley was most concerned about
avoiding a boomerang, so he took great pains to establish his
documentation and accuracy.

Examples of Quigley's paid attempt to politically assassinate Thomas are numerous. For instance, Thomas was accused of
buying a school in Connecticut in order to "educate American
youth along Russian educational ideas." Thomas was a member
of the board of trustees of a small boys school, but had re-
signed in 1946. The Utah Senator never purchased the school,
and it is impossible to imagine what that school had to do with
Communism and Utah politics.[43]

Another example of Quigley's techniques should suffice.
The Senate News headlined that "Thomas' Tariff Cut Hurt All
Utah" and then placed the effects of a free trade policy
squarely on Thomas's shoulders. According to Quigley, as a
result of the "Trade Agreements program which Senator Thomas
had initiated and supported since its inception in 1934, . . .
the country has been flooded with hundreds of millions of
dollars worth of Russian furs." This conclusion is totally
ludicrous, and this same trade policy existed throughout the
Eisenhower years. In fact, later tariff repeal was opposed
by Utah conservatives, including Senator Wallace F. Bennett.[44]

Naturally, Quigley's United States Senate News created a
statewide furor. Thomas's supporters talked of libel suits
and corrupt campaign practices. They hoped that the scandal
sheet would boomerang and cause voters to question all of the
Bennett techniques. The Democrats were destined for disappoint-
ment. Unfortunately, from Thomas's point of view, many Utahns
assumed that if there was smoke it had to be caused by fire.
A few may have actually believed the paper and concluded that
Thomas was either a fellow-traveler or a dedicated Communist.

It is also essential to realize that by late October the
senatorial campaign in Utah had become a brawl. The Democrats
published full-page newspaper advertisements that called the
Quigley charges both misleading and false. In countering all
the pro-Russian statements in Thomas's book, Four Fears, the
Democrats quoted similar statements from generals MacArthur and
Eisenhower, senators Robert A. Taft and Arthur Vandenberg,
Clare Booth Luce, and Wendell Wilkie. Logically, the ad
pointed out that all of Thomas's statements on Russia--and all
of the above Republicans' statements on Russia--were written
during World War II, when the Soviet Union was an ally of the
United States. It makes sense now, but apparently it did not
then.[45]

Wallace Bennett won decisively, and Walter Quigley claimed that his paper was the most important reason. He stated that if "properly cartooned they are picked up usually by all adult members of the family, even those on the opposite side. I have found them decisive over the years--far more than TV or radio and much cheaper. Campaign papers cannot be turned off. In 30 years of issuing them, I find they 'tip over' states within a week of their issuance."[46]

In summary of Utah's 1950 senatorial race as an example of McCarthyism: Quigley and other outsiders were hired to do a hatchet job on Senator Thomas. The charges were false and a man's political reputation was destroyed. The doubtful voter considered whether he should vote for or against Thomas, not whether he should vote for Bennett.

So the 1950 mountain states senatorial elections were over, and in both cases the incumbent was defeated. McCarthyism was a major reason that Taylor and Thomas returned to private life. McCarthyism's 1950 impact on Democratic candidates throughout the nation was significant.[47] For the next two years, McCarthy continued to accuse and attack as the nation suffered in the Korean War, tried the Rosenbergs, and prepared for atomic disaster. The year of the Eisenhower landslide, 1952, again offers an example of mountain McCarthyism.

Montana, Wyoming, and Utah all had senatorial races in 1952. In Utah, Senator Arthur V. Watkins easily won reelection over Congressman Walter Granger, and McCarthyism was never really an issue. Democratic Senator Joseph C. O'Mahoney was barely defeated in Wyoming by Governor Frank Barrett, but was a victim of the Eisenhower landslide rather than vicious charges of pro-Communism. O'Mahoney had been solidly hawkish during the Cold War and was not vulnerable on that count.[48] Montana was a different story because the outcome of the election was considered important by both parties and it both attracted McCarthy himself and suffered from McCarthyism.

Republican incumbent Zales N. Ecton was challenged by Representative Mike Mansfield, the popular First District congressman. Mansfield was an internationalist and a dedicated liberal, and had so much respect from both Roosevelt and Truman that he had a reputation as an international trouble-shooter. Ecton was an isolationist, a conservative, and a close friend of Joseph McCarthy. Rarely have voters had a better opportunity to make a real choice. Unfortunately, the issues were soon clouded by McCarthyism.[49]

Each candidate received plenty of outside help. Harry Truman came through Montana to dedicate the Hungry Horse Dam and stopped to praise Mansfield and recommend his election. Democratic presidential hopeful Adlai Stevenson also visited the big sky country, as did senators Estes Kefauver and Lester

Hill. Ecton received personal help from Dwight Eisenhower, Richard Nixon, and senators Robert Taft, Everett Dirksen, and Joseph McCarthy. The famous Republican "Truth Squad" of senators Homer Ferguson, Bourke Hickenlooper, and Francis Case visited Montana "to dispel some of the fog left in the wake of the Truman Train."[50]

Throughout the campaign Ecton continually attempted to associate Mansfield with what the Republicans referred to as "Trumanism" and softness toward Communism. The conduct of the campaign revealed very definitely an attempt to assassinate Mansfield's character by associating him with socialism and softness toward Communism which went beyond the issue. In McCarthy fashion an appeal based on the Communist issue was made to Montana voters through emotionalism and patriotism.

Ecton never called Mansfield a Communist and even said Mansfield "would not knowingly help the Communist cause," but Ecton attempted to create the belief among voters that it was Mansfield's fault China had been lost to the Communists.[51] The Republican senator attacked Mansfield's anti-Chiang Kai-shek China reports and speeches in 1944-45 and drew parallels between Mansfield's views and the views of known left-wingers and Communists on the United States China policy.[52]

A common campaign strategy employed by Ecton was to charge Mansfield with partial responsibility for the "Truman-Acheson" China policy. In Harlowton, Ecton declared:

> The China experts, including a Montana congressman (Mansfield) sent by the State Department to put pressure on Chiang Kai-shek to take Communists into his national government, were either misled into believing that these Communists were merely peaceloving agrarian reformers or they were deliberately ignoring the historic fact that Communism and government founded on Christian principles cannot be reconciled.[53]

In mid-October Senator Joseph R. McCarthy entered the Montana senatorial campaign. McCarthy's attacks on Mansfield were sufficient to remove any doubts about the use of McCarthyism in this campaign. On October 14 McCarthy addressed a crowd that so jammed an auditorium in Missoula that people were invited to take seats on the platform.[54]

McCarthy praised Senator Ecton, saying his "only crime is that he is first and last for America." He utilized the previously discussed technique of quoting from the Daily Worker, where Mansfield was praised. McCarthy dramatically stated that the Daily Worker commended Mansfield on the so-called anti-

Chiang Kai-shek report which had been made to President Roosevelt. Although McCarthy emphasized he was not accusing Mansfield of being a Communist, he declared that "a person who conducts himself so as to win the favor of the Communist party organ must be either stupid or a dupe."[55]

McCarthy was followed into Montana by Harvey M. Matusow, who supposedly represented a nonpolitical, but nevertheless deliberate, attempt to link Mansfield, the Democratic Party, and groups supporting them with Communism.[56] Matusow, a former Communist Party member, was a professional anti-Communist witness. His testimony led to numerous convictions for violation of the Smith Act. In 1952 he offered his services to McCarthy as a campaigner in Wisconsin. From there he went to Utah, Washington, and Montana, where he attempted to associate Democratic candidates with Communism. Later Matusow admitted to utilizing lies and half truths. The result of his repentance is a book, False Witness, which cannot be trusted.

Matusow claimed that McCarthy sent him to Montana to help defeat Mansfield. McCarthy told Matusow that if Mansfield were elected "you might as well have an admitted Communist in the Senate, it's the same difference."[57] So the ex-Communist was booked for a series of lectures throughout Montana. One example of Matusow's techniques should suffice.

On October 14, the Great Falls Tribune carried a paid advertisement announcing Matusow's appearance. The five-column sixteen-inch display announced that "Harvey Matusow, Communist spy for the F.B.I.," would speak in the Great Falls High School auditorium. He was sponsored and endorsed by the American Legion and the Junior Chamber of Commerce. The advertisement was indicative of McCarthyism:

> Here he is! in Great Falls . . . with the shocking truth . . . a sensational exposé of Communist activity in the U.S.
> And now the story can be told . . . former top secret stories on Communist activities in the United States are now brought to light . . . dramatic, shocking, exposing . . . the incidents as they happened . . . as they happen today. This talk is a must for everyone who holds dearly the welfare of his country.[58]

In this talk Matusow condemned many organizations as being "Red" infiltrated, including the State Department, the USO, the United Nations, the Voice of America, the Farmers Union, CBS, the YWCA, and the Boy Scouts. When questioned, he did not believe the Catholic or Mormon Churches were infiltrated, but he did say Montana had "more Communists per capita than any other state."59 He attacked Mansfield by quoting from the Daily Worker.

When Matusow left Montana, Senator Ecton picked up the gauntlet. Ecton did not believe Mansfield would knowingly aid the Communists; but, imitating McCarthy, he said, "This man who now wants to be a U.S. Senator was at least a dupe."60 The inference was that Mansfield was duped into believing the Chinese Communists were not really Communists; and, therefore, he advocated Communist-appeasing policies. According to Ecton, Mansfield was a "captive candidate of the Truman-Acheson gang who was duped by people in the State Department."61 Ecton called on Mansfield to repent, admit he had been duped and was wrong in referring to the Chinese Communists as agrarian reformers.

Apparently, Ecton believed he had successfully associated Mansfield with the "Truman-Acheson gang" in the State Department. Consequently, the viciousness of his attacks increased. Continuing to use McCarthyism, Ecton referred to the praise Mansfield had received from Truman as the result of his defense of American foreign policy against Andrei Vishinsky, Russian Foreign Minister, at a Paris meeting of the United Nations. "Mansfield," Ecton said, "should have been talking back to them [Russians] in 1944, but instead he was doing what he could to open the door to the Communists for the conquest of China."62

Ecton's campaign was belatedly aided by Richard Nixon. Nixon's original tour in Montana was intended to include stops in Missoula, Helena, Great Falls, Butte, and Billings; but because of the "fund" incident and the Checkers crisis, he canceled all the engagements except the one at Missoula. The night before he arrived in Missoula he had presented his defense of the fund over nation-wide television from Los Angeles, California. However, in November he returned to Great Falls, where he attacked the Truman administration and said Stevenson would continue the same policy because "he holds a Ph.D. degree from Acheson's school of the three C's--Cowardly Communist Containment." Also in the speech he associated Mansfield with the Truman administration and called for the election of Ecton.63

Although Mansfield was aroused, he did not retaliate directly against the charges of "Commie-Coddling" leveled against him. Rather, he campaigned on his record as a congressman and issues of economic interest to the people of Montana. Throughout the campaign he expressed his position regarding the menace of Communism and the action he had taken to combat it.

State Democratic chairman Hjalmer B. Landoe assumed the major task of retaliating against the Republican use of

McCarthyism. Early in the campaign, in an obvious reference to Ecton, he stated, "Montanans will not be stampeded by the demagoguery of an isolationist Republican senator."[64] Following McCarthy's appearance in Montana, Landoe sarcastically commented that it was "heartening" to know Mansfield was not a Communist; however, he was certain the people of Montana resented "an out-of-state smear artist--a master of the big lie and of loose talk--coming into our state and saying that one of the most conscientious and competent public servants in the history of our state is 'either stupid or a dupe.'"[65]

Although the Republicans were generally victorious in Montana and the nation in 1952, the McCarthyistic barrage against Mike Mansfield failed. The victory was not overwhelming statistically; yet Mansfield proved that McCarthyism was not a guarantee for victory in the Mountain West. The three 1954 senatorial campaigns in Montana, Idaho, and Wyoming offer further documentation.

It did not take long for Joseph McCarthy to turn on the Eisenhower administration. From his Senate position he continued to attack federal agencies, his colleagues, the State Department, and eventually the Army. It was during the 1954 Army-McCarthy hearings that the Wisconsin senator reached the end of his rope. His Senate colleagues began to exercise more control as they debated censure.[66] It is ironic that while censure of the man who left his name to the technique was being debated, McCarthyism gasped its last breath in the Rockies.

Wyoming's 1954 senatorial race was both tragic and bizarre. The Democratic incumbent, Lester C. Hunt, was a mild-mannered dentist who had also served as Wyoming's governor. After a single Senate term in which he established a liberal voting record, Hunt announced for reelection. The Republicans believed that if any other Democrat were running, they could win the seat.

On June 9, Hunt sent a startling message to the Democratic chairman of Wyoming. It was very simple: "I shall never be a candidate for elective office again. I am compelled to withdraw my announcement as a candidate for reelection."[67] Later it was announced that health was the reason for Hunt's decision, but in reality more was involved. Ever since the previous October, when his only son had been convicted of homosexual conduct, Hunt had lived in private anguish. This personal tragedy was enough cause for concern, but Hunt feared that it might be exploited politically. With Hunt out of the Senate picture, Wyoming was now considered a toss-up.

But Lester Hunt still had a tragic role to play. On July 18, McCarthy announced during the Army-McCarthy hearings that he was going to expose a senator for "just plain wrongdoing."[68] Early the next morning, Hunt went to his office in the Senate

Office Building, sat down at his desk, and shot himself in the head. Many in Washington expressed shocked regret, including South Dakota senator, Karl Mundt, chairman of McCarthy's committee during the TV hearings. Mundt assured everyone that Hunt was not the unnamed senator that McCarthy had referred to the previous day. But as one Democratic senator remarked earlier, "Every man in public life lives in a glass house. There are few if any people who haven't done something in the past that could be used against them in a political fight by an opponent wishing to bar no hold."[69]

Hunt was as vulnerable as a man could be. He was not in good health and a brother had already committed suicide. At the time, columnist Marquis Childs wrote that "Hunt's Senate foes let him know that the facts would find their way into every mailbox in Wyoming if Hunt should run for reelection this fall."[70] There is no evidence that McCarthy was personally connected with Hunt's death. However, the mood and climate created by McCarthyism may have contributed to the suicide.

With Hunt out of the picture, Wyoming's Democrats chose former senator Joseph O'Mahoney to bear their standard against Congressman William Henry Harrison, a direct descendant of the two Harrison presidents. Hunt's suicide dampened the Wyoming campaign; yet there were some feeble attempts to smear O'Mahoney as a subversive. O'Mahoney had remained in Washington after his 1952 defeat and practiced law. The Republicans attacked O'Mahoney on two counts. He was accused of being a foreign agent--in fact, foreign agent 783--because he accepted a retainer from the Cuban Sugar Council, an organization of American investors in the Cuban sugar industry. Secondly, O'Mahoney had represented Owen Lattimore, the Johns Hopkins professor accused by McCarthy of being a top Communist espionage agent. Vice-President Richard Nixon came through Wyoming and warned that the Democrats were "ignorant and blind" to the Communist issue.[71] Nixon was joined in Wyoming by President Eisenhower and Senator Everett Dirksen.

O'Mahoney claimed that he was "subjected to one of the most virulent attacks that was ever directed against a candidate, but it didn't work." In reality, it was not that vicious.[72] Throughout the campaign, O'Mahoney stressed his nineteen-year Senate record and what he could do for agriculture and water resource development. O'Mahoney won by nearly 3,500 votes and it appeared that the small-scale smear campaign backfired.[73]

Montana and Idaho were not so lucky in 1954. The senatorial elections graphically illustrated McCarthyism in operation. In Montana, Senator James Murray, who had served since 1935, was running against Wesley A. D'Ewart, a Republican Congressman. Although both candidates agreed to campaign on the current issues, it was soon apparent that the "Red Scare" was going to become the central theme.

On October 17, The New York Times contained an article entitled "Red Issue Raised to Fight Murray." The Times contended that it was a "frankly desperate" but "determined eleventh-hour campaign" on the part of the Republicans who saw no other way of defeating Murray. The Republicans circulated thousands of copies of an article entitled "A Tribute to Lenin," which Murray had written for a January 1945 issue of Soviet Russia Today. Republican party officials in the state privately deplored the use of such a tactic but viewed it as a necessity.74 It appears that D'Ewart condoned the use of these materials in view of the fact that he did not repudiate them nor those who were responsible for them.

Vice-President Nixon's speeches in Montana were typical of the national use of McCarthyism. Although he was detained in Montana by an early snowstorm, Nixon fulfilled his scheduled engagements at Billings, Butte, and Bozeman. Nixon attacked the protection given Communists and fellow travelers during the Truman administration and charged that the Communists were infiltrating the Democratic Party and controlling its policies.75 Nixon's Butte speech clearly demonstrated McCarthyism. He claimed he possessed a copy of a "secret memorandum" sent to California leaders of the Communist Party which directed them to achieve unity behind single candidates in the Democratic primaries--if possible, agreed upon in advance. The Vice-President added, "There is no question but that millions of loyal Democrats throughout the United States bitterly resent and will oppose this effort on the part of the Communists to infiltrate the Democratic party and to make its policies the policies of the Democratic party. The previous administration unfortunately adopted policies which were soft, vacillating, and inconsistent in dealing with the Communist threat."76

Whatever ethics politics may have were seriously violated with the production and distribution of "Senator Murray and the Red Web over Congress." This scurrilous attack against Murray can be described in no other way than as a deliberate attempt to deceive the voters by slurring the character of Senator Murray through irresponsible associations with Communists and Communist-front organizations. Although D'Ewart had no official connection with the publication of the booklet, he had knowledge of it.

The cover of the "Red Web" was an excellent indication of the distortions found inside. The title was in white letters in a black border across the top, and in a red border across the bottom was the statement: "The Story of Communist Infiltration of your U.S. Congress from Official Records and Communist documents." In the center was a large picture of the capitol dome with a red spider web superimposed on it. A red spider with a human head and a sinister look was located inside the web. On the web was the statement: "Read the facts."[77] The emotional appeal to patriotism is found early:

> Here is the story of the Red Web Over Congress and the activities of the aging millionaire Senator Murray of Montana. Montana citizens, remote from eastern centers of left-wing activity, have been largely unaware of the facts presented in this booklet. Few know the reputation he has acquired in the 20 years since he left Montana. Every American interested in the preservation of American liberties will find a message in these pages.[78]

Murray was accused of being the chairman or ranking Democratic member on committees which employed six staff members who, when questioned concerning Communist party affiliations, replied with the Fifth Amendment. Also, several of the six were supposedly members of Communist or Communist-front organizations with which Murray had been identified. One must question why it was implied that Murray was responsible for hiring the questionable staff members, and when and in what way Murray was identified with the Communist or Communist-front organizations. However, the effect these statements may have had on the casual but patriotic and Communist-fearing voter is obvious. The "Web" then attempted to tie Murray to Claude Pepper and claimed the House Un-American Activities Committee identified Murray with thirteen different Communist front groups. The booklet concluded:

> In this manner and for these reasons, the Communist Party from coast to coast has looked with favor on Senator James E. Murray. And this is only part of the record.
> You have read the record. You have seen the evidence. Determine for yourself whether Senator James E. Murray has represented YOU in these matters.[79]

Everything contained in the booklet claimed to be factual; at least it was thoroughly documented; but the facts were very adroitly manipulated in such a way as to turn the "Red Web" into an attempt at character assassination.

The cost of the "Red Web" must have been exceptional, but its effect was not worth the price. As a factor in the election it was probably of slight significance.

At no time during the last three weeks of the campaign was there any let-up in the attack, counter-attack, and retaliation. D'Ewart personally continued to add to the alleged association of Murray with Communism, accusing him of spending tax dollars at a Swiss resort where the "International Labor Organization meets every year."[80] In what appears to have been the script for a radio speech delivered over a Great Falls station on October 20, entitled "20 years of Murray," D'Ewart referred to his opponent as "a living relic of all that characterized the new deal days of spending, taxes, war and [Communist infiltration] corruption."[81] D'Ewart's tactics can be summed up in a statement made at Deer Lodge: "I know he [Murray] can't adequately explain his association with 13 officially designated Communist fronts, his writing a tribute to Lenin and why he voted as late as 1950 against the major legislation designed to halt Red infiltration--the U.S. national security act."[82]

Republicans were reluctant to use the name of Senator McCarthy. This is understandable because McCarthy's appeal had suffered considerably as a result of the highly publicized Army-McCarthy hearings. Finally, however, it was decided to use McCarthy but only at long range. As a result, a letter from McCarthy calling for the election of D'Ewart was received and released to the press. The letter said in part: "I do want you to know personally that I feel it would be a great victory for real Americans and for anti-Communists if Wes D'Ewart is elected."[83]

Murray defeated D'Ewart by less than 2,000 votes out of over 227,000 cast. There is a strong possibility D'Ewart would have defeated Murray had the question of "soft-on-Communism" never been noised. Some Democrats believed that if D'Ewart had run on his personal record and Eisenhower's record, it is possible he might have won without McCarthyism.[84] With it he lost.

Perhaps Idaho's 1954 Senate race offers the best example of McCarthyism in action. The political comeback of the ever vulnerable Glen Taylor was the issue. He challenged the Republican incumbent, Henry Dworshak. For most of the campaign, the two candidates discussed foreign policy, tidelands oil, and farm problems.

As mid-October approached, it seemed to some that Taylor's chances of being elected were excellent. In fact, a New York Times survey had Taylor leading Dworshak, and two weeks prior to the election Newsweek gave Taylor about a fifty-fifty chance. According to the weekly news magazine, many Idaho political experts agreed.[85] Jack Bell, an Associated Press political correspondent, called the race "a toss-up" and theorized that the last two weeks of the campaign would tell the story.[86] But in those weeks the situation changed drastically. Taylor was subjected to an extremist attack from the right which surpassed that of 1950 and even Taylor failed to prognosticate its magnitude.

Joe McCarthy's power was declining in the fall of 1954 as his Senate colleagues debated censure, but Idaho's junior Republican senator, and Taylor's personal enemy, Herman Welker, was doing his best to keep the Communism issue hot in Idaho. When Taylor heard the rumor that Welker was going to return to the Gem State to assist Dworshak, Taylor cracked: "I am particularly pleased to have Senator McCarthy's Charlie McCarthy, namely the Hon. Herman Welker, on the scene and ready to share responsibility for Henry Dworshak's forthcoming defeat."[87] Taylor knew the line Welker would take and he simply stated before Welker even returned to Idaho: "The Republicans are going to say Glen Taylor is a Communist. They are going to smear me as a Red."[88] Henry Dworshak, the candidate for re-election, took a seat on the sidelines as Welker went to work on Taylor.

Welker called a special subcommittee of McCarthy's infamous Senate Internal Security Subcommittee into secret session in early October. Oddly, it was a one-man subcommittee because Welker was the lone senator in attendance. Later, Taylor referred to Welker's subcommittee as a "secret, one man hearing in a phone booth."[89] Welker paraded before himself Herbert Philbrick, Matthew Cvetic, John Lautner, and other former FBI agents who had posed as Communists. The supposedly significant revelation which came out of the hearings was that Wallace and Taylor knew the Communists were aiding the Progressive party in 1948.[90]

Cvetic vividly recalled being in meetings where Taylor and Wallace made remarks to the effect that "they welcomed the vote of anyone."[91] This was certainly true. For instance, Taylor had made it clear when he faced the reporters after announcing his decision to join Wallace, but he also stated that his goal was to make the system work so well that Communism would have no appeal to mass America.[92] This statement was not remembered by the former FBI agents. In the paranoid hysteria of the early fifties, Welker's alleged findings were treated as new discoveries.

Lautner and Cvetic also accused the Progressive candidates of knowing that the party was under Communist control and that Wallace and Taylor were hand picked by the Communists because they were "two men who were willing to work with the Communist party in the coalition Progressive party."[93] It was Lautner's contention that a former Vice-President, Wallace, and a United States senator, Taylor, had the effect of "giving respectability to the Communist cause."[94]

Herb Philbrick's "I Led Three Lives" was currently a popular television program and Matt Cvetic's "I Was a Communist for the FBI" had recently enjoyed tremendous radio success. This was tough company for former Senator Taylor; and the informers, with Welker's assistance, had released enough clouded information to destroy a bevy of politicians. Yet Glen Taylor refused to roll over for the onslaught.

Upon discovering the Welker hearings, Taylor immediately telegraphed Welker and challenged Idaho's junior senator to subpoena Taylor prior to the election. Taylor demanded that the hearing be held in Idaho, with both politicans represented by legal counsel, and that Taylor's counsel have the privilege of cross-examining all of Welker's previous witnesses. The Democratic candidate also suggested that Welker owed it to the people of Idaho to take the stand and submit to examination.[95]

Welker called Taylor's challenge "a grandstand play," but did promise to call Taylor before the subcommittee at the earliest possible time. Welker and Taylor exchanged telegrams of charges and counter-charges as the election date neared. Finally Welker stated that Taylor had belatedly asked for the hearing and that it could not be organized at such a late date.[96] Henry Wallace offered to testify that the Progressive party was never controlled by one political ideology or faction, but he was not summoned.[97]

After the possibility of hearings conducted in Idaho faded into unreality, Welker resumed his bitter assault on Taylor and the latter's association with the 1948 Progressives:

> I would like to give Glen Taylor a break and say that he was merely a dupe and a stooge . . . , but I would not insult his intelligence by suggesting that he was so stupid as to fail to recognize his bedfellows in red flannels. If he was that stupid he doesn't deserve to be United States Senator.[98]

With that utterance, Welker went to Oregon for two days to harass the Democratic senatorial candidate there, Richard Neuberger.

Welker persuaded Matt Cvetic to join him in Idaho and scheduled a speaking tour for the former FBI agent. While Cvetic toured traditionally Democratic northern Idaho speaking on the threat of a Communist takeover, Welker followed Vice-President Nixon, Senator Barry Goldwater of Arizona, Secretary of Agriculture Ezra T. Benson, Speaker of the House Joseph Martin of Massachusetts, and Senator Everett M. Dirksen of Illinois through southern Idaho.

Reacting poorly to Cvetic's presence in the state, Taylor accused the former agent of selling his services to the highest bidder. He stated that Cvetic was "taking advantage of the fertile field cultivated by the hysterical political campaign to collect handsome fees from desperate Republicans."99 During these days of militant fearful anti-Communism, Cvetic's answers cost Taylor votes. At Kellogg, Cvetic said he had been called such names many times, always by the Communist Daily Worker and thousands of other Communists. Concluding his speech, Cvetic made an effective plea:

> If serving my country by posing as a Communist for the FBI for nine heartbreaking years during which my mother died believing I had betrayed her adopted country makes me what Glen Taylor and the Communist party say I am, then my only answer to them is that I am proud to have had an opportunity to serve my country.100

In all probability, Cvetic hurt Taylor more than Welker did, in part because Taylor degraded himself to attacking personalities in replying to the Cvetic charges.

The activity of Vice-President Nixon typified the billowing anti-Taylor smokescreen devised to confuse the Idaho electorate late in the campaign. The primary function of Nixon's western tour was to defeat Democratic senatorial candidates in Wyoming, Colorado, Oregon, and Montana, as well as Taylor in Idaho. Using scare tactics and half-truths, Nixon attempted to win a greater Republican majority for Eisenhower in the senate. According to the vice-president, the Communist party was fighting desperately for the election of an anti-Eisenhower congress. He also stated the western Democrats belonged to a "left-wing" clique in their party which had tolerated the "Red conspiracy."101

Nixon told a gathering at the Pocatello High School auditorium, "Taylor's record is so well known in Idaho that I don't think any comment from me is necessary." Then he did comment: "Taylor is dedicated to a political philosophy opposite from that of the people of Idaho who voted two-to-one for Ike in 1952."102 Once the former California senator was in gear, there was no stopping him. He had discovered a secret memorandum showing that the Communists planned to conduct their program within the Democratic party. On 23 January 1953, three days after Ike's inauguration, Nixon had allegedly found in the files left behind by the Democrats a blueprint for socializing America. Why he waited until the off-year election of 1954 to reveal such startling evidence, Mr. Nixon did not say.103 Also stating that the Republicans had fired 6,926 federal employees as security risks, Nixon warned that "if the left-wing gets back into power, these discharged security risks will get back their jobs."[104]

As Taylor attempted to emerge from the rhetorical hurricane engulfing him, he discovered the opposition wanted to destroy him totally and eternally. Perhaps the weirdest and most startling development of the final hectic week was the sudden accusation, four years after Taylor had left the Senate, that Glen Taylor had hired Communists to work for him in his Senate office. One of his former employees, Ross Haworth, visiting in Idaho, made the charge four days prior to the election. Haworth, who had been fired by Taylor in 1946, specifically accused Taylor of accepting money from an alleged ex-Communist, John Abt; of making overtures to Harry Bridges, president of the Longshoreman's Union; and of having no interest in Idaho's needs and problems.[105]

Still Taylor was subjected to one final vicious attack. Two days prior to the election, Herman Welker returned to the state and he "now had Taylor cold." According to Welker, Taylor had affiliated himself with three organizations that were on the Attorney General's list of subversive groups. Citing the American Committee for Yugoslav Relief, the Congress of Civil Rights, and the Independent Committee of the Arts, Sciences, and Professions, Welker concluded that Taylor's "collaboration with Communists and Communist-fronts was by no means limited to his vice-presidential candidacy on the Progressive ticket in 1948."[106] At one time in his career, Taylor had addressed all of the above liberal organizations. The groups had been nearly unanimous in their support for the Progressives and of course their existence was not even a reality for most Idahoans. All Welker needed was to have someone pore through the pages of the *Daily Worker* and ferret out all favorable references to Taylor.

Suffering one of the worst defeats in Idaho political history, Taylor simply stated, "I do believe that the last-minute smear which came too late for an effective rebuttal is largely responsible for the outcome of the election."[107] Dworshak defeated Taylor by approximately 60,000 votes. It was a bitter pill to swallow for a man who two weeks earlier was judged as even in the polls.

Taylor, permanently retired to private life, would have agreed with Adlai E. Stevenson's assessment of the 1954 Republican assault on the West. Referring to the entire political scene as "McCarthyism in a white collar," the former Illinois governor scored Nixon in particular. "Under the boisterous leadership of the nation's vice-president, the Republican high command chose to make this 1954 campaign not a testing ground for ideas, not a forum for that debate which is democracy's sole source of strength, but rather a cheap, sordid ugly feat of slogans, charges and epithets."108 President Dwight Eisenhower praised Nixon for a "tremendous job" and further stated that "no man could have done more effective work than you to further the GOP chances."109 It is ironic to note that the Democrats recaptured both the Senate and the House in 1954, so apparently without Nixon's assistance, the Republicans might have suffered an even more devastating defeat. Or perhaps Eisenhower was being cynical--but that is doubtful.

Nationally the GOP and Nixon were out of touch with the mood of the country: the Democrats recaptured the Congress. Nevertheless, it is difficult to change some men's methods and styles. The New Republic sarcastically stated that Mr. Nixon would not rest until Harry Truman was out of the White House and Alger Hiss was safely in jail.110 Or, as an editorial stated after the election: "The one stroke of misfortune that we can all pray will not occur is for Dicky Nixon to become President."111

In conclusion, McCarthyism in the Mountains transcended the man. In the six cases studied, the technique only succeeded three times and in at least two of those three there were many other reasons to explain defeat. Yet the very fact that McCarthyism was such a prominent tactic merits the study. Its effects were witnessed in Congress, courts, churches, schools, the press, libraries, the entertainment industry, and all levels of government. By fear and innuendo, many lives were wrongfully destroyed. We know why it happened and we can speculate that some form of McCarthyism will return. It is most confusing to attempt to predict when, but perhaps Lewis Carroll in Through the Looking Glass provides the most plausible explanation:

> "I see nobody on the road," said Alice.
> "I only wish I had such eyes," the King remarked in a fretful tone. "To be able to see Nobody! And at that distance too!"

REFERENCES

1. For reasons of length and cohesiveness, the author has chosen to define the Mountain West as Idaho, Montana, Utah, and Wyoming. This may be a geographical error, but the purposes of the paper are better served by this definition.

2. Robert Griffith and Athan Theoharis, eds., The Specter: Original Essays on the Cold War and the Origins of McCarthyism (New York: New Viewpoints, 1974), pp. 9-13.

3. Robert Griffith, The Politics of Fear: Joseph R. McCarthy and the Senate (Lexington: University of Kentucky Press, 1970), pp. 30-51.

4. On the entire issue of the Truman response, see Athan Theoharis, Seeds of Repression: Harry S. Truman and the Origins of McCarthyism (Chicago: Quadrangle, 1971).

5. Griffith and Theoharis, The Specter, pp. 16-17.

6. For a full discussion of Taylor's career, see F. Ross Peterson, Prophet Without Honor: Glen H. Taylor and the Fight for American Liberalism (Lexington: University of Kentucky Press, 1974).

7. United States Congressional Record, 81st Cong., 2nd Sess., 1950, v. 96, pt. 13: A 1405-6.

8. Lewiston Morning Tribune, 15 May 1950.

9. Glen H. Taylor's Record on Foreign Affairs, Glen H. Taylor File, CIO-PAC Research Department, Washington, D.C.

10. Idaho State Journal, 26 June 1950.

11. Ibid., 7 July 1950. See also Lewiston Morning Tribune, 9 July 1950; Idaho Daily Statesman, 9 July 1950.

12. Lewiston Morning Tribune, 1 August 1950. The China Lobby was a group supporting Chiang Kai-shek who attempted to persuade the United States to give Chiang massive financial and military assistance.

13. Ibid., 3 August 1950.

14. Idaho State Journal, 5 July 1950.

15. Ibid., 27 July 1950.

16. Lewiston Morning Tribune, 2 August 1950.

17. Idaho State Journal, 4 August 1950.

18. Idaho Daily Statesman, 25 July 1950.

19. Interview with John Corlett, 14 September 1967. The owners of the Idaho Daily Statesman, Margaret Cobb Ailshie and James Brown, were convinced that Taylor and his senatorial office were being used by the Communists.

20. Idaho Daily Statesman, 2 July 1950.

21. Ibid., 24 July 1950. The series on Taylor and Pepper was carried throughout July and up to the primary election. The editorials appeared almost daily.

22. Ibid., 6 July 1950.

23. Ibid., 29 July 1950. The three Democrats were C. E. Brown of McCall, P. C. O'Malley of Pocatello, and Frank McCall of Salem.

24. Ibid., 27 July 1950.

25. Ibid., 30 July 1950.

26. Ibid., 24 April 1949.

27. Ibid., 6 August 1950.

28. Ibid.

29. Ibid.

30. Clark received 26,897 to Taylor's 25,949. Compton White, a former congressman from Northern Idaho, obtained 14,599. It was a heavy turnout for an Idaho off-year election, but even if he had won the primary it would have taken a miracle for Taylor to win the general election.

31. Idaho Daily Statesman, 13 August 1954. See also the same paper for August 11, 1950.

32. Ibid., 28 May 1950.

33. Lewiston Morning Tribune, 11 August, 1950.

34. There are three major sources on Elbert D. Thomas's 1950 election. All of them are authored by Frank H. Jonas, a University of Utah political scientist. They can be found in "The 1950 Elections in Utah," The Western Political Science Quarterly, 4(1951):81-91; "The Mormon Church and Political Dynamiting in the 1950 Election in Utah," Proceedings of the Utah Academy of Sciences, Arts, and Letters, 40, part 1 (1963): 94-110; and Political Dynamiting (Salt Lake City: University of Utah Press, 1970), pp. 47-108; also, of course, Thomas's own papers.

35. An adequate discussion of the factors that contributed to Thomas's defeat is found in Jonas, "The 1950 Elections in Utah," pp. 83-84.

36. Jonas, Political Dynamiting, contains a copy of the leaflet (p. 75), and this discussion is based on that copy and its circulation. Included on the list were Louis Adamic, William Rose Benet, Mary McLeod Bethune, Van Wyck Brooks, Theodore Dreiser, Lena Horne, George Gessel, Carey McWilliams, Hazel Scott, and Max Weber.

37. Ibid.

38. Jonas, Political Dynamiting, p. 76. Allen distributed considerable amounts of right-wing literature. They were invariably antiblack and anti-Semitic.

39. Jonas, "The 1950 Election in Utah," pp. 89-90; Political Dynamiting contains a complete and detailed description of the newspaper, pp. 83-97.

40. Jonas, Political Dynamiting, p. 89.

41. Ibid.

42. Ibid.

43. Ibid., p. 90.

44. Ibid., pp. 93-94.

45. Salt Lake Tribune, 27 October 1950.

46. Walter Quigley to Frank Jonas, 13 November 1955, quoted in Jonas, Political Dynamiting, p. 104. Quigley's claims cannot be sustained or disputed. There were several other issues involved, including the AMA-sponsored attacks because Thomas was for a national health insurance. What may have had a greater impact was that many in Thomas's church, the LDS Church, turned on him during the final days of the campaign. A sheet was circulated by prominent Church members that suggested Thomas was for gambling, prostitution, and drinking. Those charges could shoot down a flock of candidates in Utah. See Jonas, "The Mormon Church and Political Dynamiting in Utah." These accusations cut Thomas deeply and disillusioned him about politics in Utah.

47. Richard M. Fried, "Electoral Politics and McCarthyism: The 1950 Campaign," in Griffith and Theoharis, The Specter, pp. 190-222.

48. F. Alan Coombs is completing a biography of Joseph C. O'Mahoney and kindly sent me copies of numerous documents bearing on the 1952 campaign. Said Coombs, "I must confess to a certain amount of surprise that McCarthyism and the 'Communists-in-government' issue did not play a prominent role in this campaign; Wyoming Republicans of that era were certainly capable of playing that theme for all it was worth" (F. Alan Coombs to author, 9 September 1974). Coombs speculates that O'Mahoney was overconfident and had lost touch with Wyoming, but that the real reason for O'Mahoney's defeat was the massive majorities rolled up by Eisenhower. He had 63 percent of Wyoming's vote and O'Mahoney had 49 percent.

49. William D. Miller, "Montana and the Specter of McCarthyism, 1952-54," master's thesis, Montana State University, 1969. This is a very fine thesis and was of great assistance.

50. Billings Gazette, 2 October 1952.

51. Ibid., 18 October 1952.

52. Jules A. Karlin, "The 1952 Elections in Montana," The Western Political Quarterly, 61:115-16.

53. Great Falls Tribune, 4 October 1952.

54. Daily Missoulian, 15 October 1952.

55. Great Falls Tribune, 15 October 1952.

56. Harvey Matusow, False Witness (New York: Cameron and Kohn, 1955).

57. Ibid., p. 156.

58. Great Falls Tribune, 14 October 1952.

59. Ibid., 15 October 1952.

60. Billings Gazette, 18 October 1952.

61. Great Falls Tribune, 22 October 1952.

62. Billings Gazette, 23 October 1952.

63. Great Falls Tribune, 2 November 1952.

64. Ibid., 10 October 1952.

65. Ibid., 16 October 1952.

66. Griffith, Politics of Fear, is an excellent, well-documented account of the McCarthy-Senate relationship.

67. Washington Post, 10 June 1954.

68. Ibid., 19 June 1954.

69. New York Times Magazine, 12 April 1953, p. 28.

70. Washington Post, 30 June 1954.

71. T. A. Larson, History of Wyoming (Lincoln: University of Nebraska Press, 1965), pp. 520-21.

72. U.S. News and World Report, 37:75-76.

73. Herman H. Trachsel, "The 1954 Election in Wyoming," Western Political Quarterly, 7, no. 4:633-36.

74. New York Times, 17 October 1954.

75. Great Falls Tribune, 23 October 1954.

76. Ibid.

77. "Senator Murray and the Red Web over Congress," pamphlet, James E. Murray Collection, University of Montana, Missoula, Montana.

78. Ibid., p. 3

79. Ibid., p. 24.

80. Billings Gazette, 13 October 1954.

81. Paper entitled: "20 Years of Murray," Wesley A. D'Ewart papers, University of Montana, Missoula, Montana.

82. Lewiston Daily News, 29 October 1954.

83. Great Falls Tribune, 27 October 1954.

84. Thomas Payne, "The 1954 Elections in Montana," The Western Political Quarterly, 7, No. 4:611.

85. New York Times, 4 October 1954; "Let 'Em Wail," Newsweek, 25 October 1954, p. 31.

86. Idaho Daily Statesman, 22 October 1954.

87. Lewiston Morning Tribune, 30 August 1954.

88. New York Times, 11 October 1954.

89. Lewiston Morning Tribune, 21 October 1954.

90. U.S. Senate Subcommittee to Investigate the Administration of the Internal Security Act and Other Internal Security Laws, Hearings, Communist Propaganda, 83rd Cong., 2nd Sess., 1954, pts. 1-3. Hereafter cited as Hearings, Communist Propaganda.

91. Ibid.

92. Spokane Spokesman-Review, 24 February 1948.

93. Hearings, Communist Propaganda.

94. Ibid.

95. Lewiston Morning Tribune, 22 October 1954; Idaho Daily Statesman, 22 October 1954.

96. Lewiston Morning Tribune, 23 October 1954.

97. New York Times, 21 October 1954.

98. Idaho Daily Statesman, 27 October 1954.

99. *Lewiston Morning Tribune*, 28 October 1954.

100. Ibid.

101. *Washington Post*, 24 October 1954.

102. *Idaho Daily Statesman*, 26 October 1954.

103. "On the Last Lap: The GOP Runs Wild," *New Republic*, 1 October 1954, pp. 3-4.

104. *Idaho Daily Statesman*, 26 October 1954.

105. *Lewiston Morning Tribune*, 30 October 1954.

106. *Lewiston Morning Tribune*, 31 October 1954.

107. Ibid., 3 November 1954.

108. *Washington Post*, 24 October 1954.

109. Ibid., 29 October 1954.

110. "On the Last Lap: GOP Runs Wild," *New Republic*, p. 4.

111. "Washington Wire," Ibid., p. 2.

Social Accommodation in Utah
Clark S. Knowlton

The accommodation of subgroups has been of constant concern in the development of the United States. Here, Clark S. Knowlton, professor of sociology and director of social research at the American West Center at the University of Utah, has posed a number of questions dealing with the problems of accommodating Anglo-American Mormon culture to the cultural traditions of minority groups in the western United States and Latin America.

It should be noted that some efforts have already been made to answer several of the questions which Professor Knowlton has posed. Dennis Lythgoe and Jan Shipps, for instance, have done considerable work on the public image of Mormonism and have presented a number of papers on the subject. Dr. Shipps is currently at work on a monographic study. In addition, articles dealing with cultural conflict in the development of the LDS Church have been published in such periodicals as Dialogue, BYU Studies, and the Journal of Mormon History.

Beyond this, a number of the volumes in the sesquicentennial history of the Church now in preparation will deal with Mormon society and the interaction of Mormonism with Latin American and other cultural groups. F. Lamond Tullis, for instance, has been at work on the interaction of Anglo-American and Latin American. On the problem of political accommodation, studies by Klaus Hansen, Gustive Larson, Leo Lyman, and others have already produced significant results. John Sorenson's work on the process of social accommodation has provided understanding, and Helen Z. Papanikolas is currently editing an ethnic history of Utah which should provide insights into intercultural relationships.

Perhaps the most significant contribution of Professor Knowlton's essay is his analysis of the process of dealing with political and social issues and his insights into the strengths and weaknesses of the system. As he has indicated, in Utah strident activism has tended to be ignored. Unfortunately, the failure to recognize the legitimacy of active protest has led to the failure to deal with such important needs as public housing and land use planning. In other words, Utahns have paid a price for political peace--often in the form of excessive costs at some distance down the road for the failure to face up to present needs.

Accommodation is defined by sociologists as the social process through which conflict and competition between individuals and groups within a society are regulated in such a way that social peace is preserved and maintained. The social processes of competition and conflict have positive social functions. Through competition, individuals and groups work harder, produce more, and tend to excel. Conflict between individuals and groups may release social tensions and strains, strengthen group unity, reveal the presence of underlying social problems and conflicting issues, and clear the social atmosphere. Uncontrolled, however, these same processes may lead to the erosion of social unity and the breakdown of law and order.[1]

Thus, accommodation diminishes tension, socializes and regulates conflict, and defines acceptable patterns of competition. These accommodative processes do not necessarily resolve issues or disputes, and may break down if social tensions become so strong and resultant conflicts between groups so widespread that existing social mechanisms and processes are not strong enough to contain them. Then widespread civil disorders or even civil war develop, through which issues are resolved by force and violence.[2]

Accommodative adjustments range over a wide area of possible social relations. As a result of conflict, one group may be able to enforce its will over other groups, reducing them to a position of social, economic, or political subordination. This process is often called superordination-subordination. At times it may not be possible for one group to achieve a definite position of strength over other groups without having to pay an unacceptable price. The two groups at conflict may then try to reach a compromise in which each group receives enough to cause it to support the compromise temporarily or permanently.

If such a compromise or truce is impossible to work out and the groups at issue are still not willing to pay the price of open conflict, they may decide to tolerate each other. Toleration is a process through which groups who do not accept each other's values, life styles, or political, economic, or social institutions ignore the differences for the sake of social peace.[3]

These and other forms of accommodation may be found in every society. The cultural values, the socioeconomic characteristics, and the patterns of social interaction between individuals and social groups determine the importance, the form, and the function that each type of accommodation may have in a given society.

Not all members of a society or even their leaders necessarily understand the accommodative processes in their society. Thus, in the United States, many people tend to assume that prices today are set through open competition in the marketplace through the workings of the free enterprise system. In effect, however, prices tend to be set by large corporations at the level that will give them the desired profit regardless of the actual costs of production. The prices of most appliances and goods we buy are rarely established by the forces of competition in the marketplace. Corporations come together legally or illegally to regulate competition, set prices, and divide markets. Price levels are also deeply influenced by the actions of our own and of foreign governments to control the movement of goods and currencies. To say today, then, that competition sets prices through the free workings of the marketplace is to be blind to political and economic realities.

Research into the existing accommodative processes of a society may provide us with considerable data and insight into the society's structure and processes. More specifically, such research may help us to understand the patterns of competition, conflict, and cooperation between individuals and groups within a society. We are informed how a society is put together and how it functions. Furthermore, a knowledge of the processes of accommodation in our own society can help us to better understand ourselves, where we have been, and where we may be going. This knowledge of our society is one of the major goals of all of the social sciences.

This presentation will focus upon certain selected aspects of the processes of accommodation in Utah, as they affect both Mormons and non-Mormons, with occasional side glimpses of other areas. I would like not only to call attention to major aspects of these relationships, but also to indicate what I consider are areas in which research is badly needed. It is, of course, far easier to ask questions than it is to answer them. Unfortunately, however, so little research has been done in terms of sociological analyses of accommodation in Utah and between non-Mormons and Mormons that perhaps you will forgive me for concentrating perhaps more on questions and less on answers.

Furthermore, I should point out that I have, like many social scientists, developed certain biases and highly personal orientations from my own work in the area of accommodation and acculturation of minority groups, primarily in the Southwest. The conclusions that I present here are highly tentative and subject to future revision. I would like to invite you to challenge my statements and conclusions, to disagree with me, and to ask whatever questions you desire. To some degree all of us are seekers after knowledge in a joint endeavor to understand ourselves, our past, and perhaps our future a little better.

The state of Utah provides an ideal social laboratory in which to study the processes of group competition, conflict, cooperation, compromise, and accommodation. Few states have had such a unique history as Utah has had. Although first settled by the American Indians and explored by Spaniards, Mexicans, and Mexican Americans, Utah became the home of a specific group of Americans, the Mormons fleeing from religious persecution on the Missouri and Illinois frontier. Here they secured an isolated refuge that permitted them to create their own society without hindrance for several decades. The structure of Mormon culture built during this period has been strong enough to resist whatever political, economic, or cultural assaults have been made against it. The Mormons still dominate Utah culturally and, presumably, politically, although the percentage of the state population that is Mormon has decreased somewhat since the 1940s.

Even though the Mormons are drawing more scholarly interest from all branches of the social sciences today than they have in the past, one issue important at least to sociologists and anthropologists remains embarrassingly unresolved. That is, what exactly are the Mormons? They are a most difficult people to define neatly and precisely. They simply do not fit comfortably into any of the definitions that have been devised by scholars to categorize and to classify human groups. And yet definition is rather important. The names that people prefer to be called reflect not only their self-image but also the image that they would like to have in a society. Such names also reflect the attitudes of outsiders toward the group and define the group's position in the social, ethnic, and racial class structure. Names and definitions are therefore rather important socially and also in scholarly discourse. Before one can hope to properly study a group of people, it is essential to give them a name.

The Mormons view themselves as belonging to the only true church of Christ on the face of the earth at the present time--a church founded on revelation received by the martyred prophet, Joseph Smith. Many Mormons may not be fully aware of the cultural or social implications of their claims or of the way that these claims are viewed by others. Some non-Mormons consider Mormonism one of the many poorly defined religious sects located on the fringes of Christianity but well outside the mainstream, while others place Mormonism among the major Christian denominations--but with a few peculiar theological traits. Still other non-Mormons argue that Mormonism simply does not fall into the accepted definition of a Christian denomination because of its centralized organization, its concern with social and economic issues, many of its past theological principles, such as polygyny, that differed considerably from common Christian standards, and its intense social unity.

For example, some of my non-Mormon colleagues at the University of Utah classify themselves as "Mormon watchers." Fascinated by Mormon behavior and culture, they observe Mormons as though they were a unique species of men and argue and speculate endlessly among themselves what Mormonism is all about. I have heard some of them argue that Mormonism, with its strongly centralized, hierarchical ecclesiastical organization built on the basis of a highly localized, decentralized stake and ward system and its welfare program, is in reality a government and even a society in embryo that once knew considerable independence and could again become operational as an autonomous society in a period of social or political chaos.

They also listen to Latter-day Saint preaching about the coming of the end of the world. They hear Mormons talk about the terrible tribulations that will afflict mankind: the natural calamities, the endless wars, and the breaking of nations. They claim that many Mormons are more fascinated and interested in the terrible events that presumably must precede the coming of Christ than they are in the coming itself. Some of them state that this may be a subconscious reflection of a suppressed Mormon desire to establish a fully autonomous, if not independent, society. Thus they consider us to be a cell within the larger social structure that is the United States, that under certain social circumstances could become an independent society itself. They speak of submerged Mormon nationalism--whatever that may mean.

Other Mormon watchers define Mormons as not only a religious minority, but also an ethnic minority. Here it should be pointed out that an ethnic group is a group whose culture, language, or dialect is distinguishably different from that of the dominant group in a society. The dominant group in the United States, of course, are the white, middle-class, Protestant, English-speaking Americans.[4] These watchers are not sure that Mormons necessarily share or accept the value systems, in spite of the very observable patriotism and identification with the United States as a nation. I have heard some of my colleagues argue strongly that Mormons are but superficially Americanized, and that under this veneer of urbanized materialistic Americanism are to be found Mormon values that are quite different from those of middle-class Anglo-America. And I have listened to other Mormon watchers observe that, fundamentally, Mormons share the basic values of Anglo-America, differing from it only in superficials. Thus a considerable amount of confusion exists over efforts by non-Mormons to define Mormons. Apparently few Mormons have entered into the game of self-definition, but it is an interesting one that has considerable significance.

Thus those that claim that Latter-day Saints are in reality an ethnic group emphasize that Mormons behave like members of an ethnic group. They encourage their young people to marry within the group. They tend to socialize almost exclusively with their fellow Mormons. Their lives are encompassed by church activities to such an extent that they are not as active as non-Mormons in national civic, social, or fraternal organizations. They also point out that when Mormons migrate from the Mormon communities of the west they tend to locate as close to Mormon chapels as possible. They prefer to interact socially with Mormons and often have few deeper than business and professional relationships with non-Mormons. They patronize Mormon businessmen and professionals and are seldom active in local political, social, cultural, or fraternal organizations. It is also observed that many of these Mormons are extremely anxious to return to their native communities, even though it may mean a substantial loss in living standards and professional careers.

I have even heard a few claim that at one time Mormons were a distinct minority, ethnic or religious, but that over the years they have acculturated into middle-class Anglo-American culture as a result of persistent and harsh religious, political, and economic pressures. Mormons, in order to free themselves from these pressures and to win acceptance from non-Mormons, were willing to rid themselves of many if not all of the unique Mormon values that they once possessed, so they say.

The basic issue, of course, is how Mormons define themselves and how they are defined by the majority of their fellow Americans. If Mormons define themselves as being but a segment of middle-class Anglo-America, then they will have a tendency to adopt middle-class Anglo-American values, to pretend that conflicts between Mormon and middle-class American values do not exist, and perhaps even to slowly lose whatever unique values Mormons may have had. On the other hand, if Mormons were to define themselves now or at some future date as an ethnic or even a religious minority, then they might assume that Mormon values are different from those of other Americans and perhaps attempt to study and to elucidate Mormon and non-Mormon values. They might even be led to assess their economic, political, and minority position in American society.

If other Americans define Mormons as but one of the numerous religious denominations in middle-class American society, then they may be shocked or surprised if Mormons do not behave as other Americans of the same social class are expected to behave. They may also react with some hostility at Mormon efforts to maintain such boundary mechanisms as in-group marriage. On the other hand, if Americans of this social class were to define Mormons as a unique religious or ethnic minority quite distinct from dominant Anglo-American middle-class society, then they may require Mormons to behave like members of an ethnic minority and force Mormons to consider how Mormons might best preserve their group identity and their distinctive socioeconomic and religious characteristics in modern society. These are questions that apparently have not troubled the Mormon intelligentsia, but perhaps it might be pointed out that Mormon adjustment to American society is and has always been an uneasy one, with many muted tones in these days of reserve and some questioning hostility as well as respect and admiration.

It is my impression that the question of definition is becoming more important among young Mormon students. Troubled as they are, like many American students many are no longer sure of what they really are. They have little knowledge of Mormon history. At best they possess some scraps of Mormon theology and history acquired from Sunday School and seminary classes. They sense in rather a confused way that they do differ in some fundamental ways from their non-Mormon friends, but tend to define these differences in terms of the Word of Wisdom, dating practices, and moral behavior. Many, because of a weak Mormon identity, drift away into inactivity or abandon Mormonism for some other religious or political ideology, totally unaware of the rich and complex although relatively unknown Mormon heritage in social experimentation, regional and urban planning, cooperation, conservation, attitudes toward animal life, towards nature, and towards the role of man in the universe, differential definitions of the good life, and mutually satisfying ways in which men may relate to each other--all areas of great interest to many young Mormons.

I have also sensed a really deep, unfed hunger among many Mormon people, young and old, for more knowledge about their own heritage. They really want to know who they are and what they are. They desire to belong to a functioning religious or social community as a defense against what to many of them is an aimless, meaningless existence in a harsh world where they have no control or sense of belonging. As I see it, one of the duties of Mormon scholarship is to feed this hunger by providing Mormons a knowledge of their history, an understanding of their culture, and a precise delineation of similarities and differences between Mormon and non-Mormon values and behavior patterns. Latter-day Saints need intellectual and cultural feeding as well as material nourishment. To understand ourselves, we must know what we are and what we are not.

A side reflection on this question of identity is the Mormon image in the mass media of television, radio, newspapers, and magazines. Has anyone studied the tone of comments about us in Time, Newsweek, Cosmopolitan, and other mass subscription magazines and in the scholarly journals? Is our public image more or less favorable than it was say ten, twenty, thirty, or forty years ago? If it is changing, then what are the factors responsible? Can Mormons influence the image that others may have about them? We should monitor our public image as it definitely affects the way that the world will behave toward us and the success of our missionary program.

As we look at the problem of Mormon identity in the United States, perhaps we ought to consider Mormonism on the world stage. Missionaries are now working in an ever-increasing number of foreign countries. As Mormon missionaries leave the United States, they carry with them an invisible luggage of not only Mormon values but also middle-class Anglo-American values. As converts are made, missionaries often subconsciously convert them not only to Mormonism but also to middle-class Americanism. Church members in foreign countries sense the often negative attitudes toward their culture on the part of missionaries who usually know little about the members' culture or history. Respecting and loving the missionaries, accepting what they say as truth and modeling their behavior upon that of the missionaries, they may come to view their own society and culture through the eyes of the missionaries, especially if they come from the lower socioeconomic levels of society with little knowledge of the complex systems of their own culture. They thus may become marginal both to their own culture and to that of the United States, unable to function fully in either.[5]

Having lived in several Latin American countries for prolonged periods of time as a missionary, as a student, and as a professional worker, I am persuaded that the above analysis is true. My impression is that as Mormonism becomes a worldwide religion the Church members must disentangle the basic principles of the gospel from American culture and separate the two. Mormon missionaries and members should skillfully try to insert basic Mormon beliefs into local cultural systems until Mormonism comes to be defined as part of the local cultural scene. Mormonism defined as Brazilian, Argentine, Spanish, Italian, or Korean may be accepted and even encouraged in those countries. Through the appointing of local leaders as bishops and stake presidents Mormons have an advantage over many Protestant denominations that rely upon missionaries from the United States and Europe to provide leadership to foreign missions. On the other hand, if Mormonism is defined as American it may come under increasing attack, as anti-Americanism unfortunately seems to be on the increase in many sections of the world.

Nationalism is on the rise everywhere in Asia, Africa, and Latin America, and if Mormonism can successfully become a basic component of many diverse cultures in different stages of social and economic development it may spread faster and be more acceptable than if it is viewed as an American import bringing in many questionable American values and behavior patterns to threaten the integrity of the local culture or be offensive to local moral behavior. Perhaps the very reason why Mormon missionaries surprisingly enough have escaped attack in countries where terrorism is becoming a problem and American businessmen and diplomatic representatives face the danger of kidnaping and murder is that the terrorists do not define Mormonism as necessarily foreign or American.[6]

Social mobility and cultural integration of Mormon converts in their own societies is another aspect of the accommodative process that we ought to examine. I have noticed in Latin America that many Mormon and Protestant converts from lower socioeconomic groups, after conversion, modify their life patterns. Acquiring traditional Protestant and Mormon attitudes toward hard work and thrift; abstaining from such money-consuming activities as smoking, drinking, and carousing; and focusing upon the family, they become valuable employees and in time move up the socioeconomic ladder, saving their money and educating their children. They expand the size of the local middle class.

However, as they or their children move up into the upper social levels, as defined by the local society, certain problems may develop. Such upper social classes are apt to be more Catholic than the more insecure, recently developed middle class or the poor rural peasants or urban workers. Because of the Roman Catholic orientation of traditional upper-class elites and more recently arrived business and political elites, Mormon and Protestant upwardly mobile individuals and families often come under social pressure to abandon their Mormonism or Protestantism and become Roman Catholics. Finding their professional, business, intellectual, or social progress hampered by their religion, they may be tempted to abandon it for Catholicism, or for some foreign ideology, such as one of the many forms of debased Marxism floating around Latin America. As the educational levels of more and more Mormon families in Latin America improve, they will inevitably move up the class ladder. What can the Mormon Church do to help them in their upward mobility while assisting them to resist pressures toward Catholicism from the dominant elite?[7]

A somewhat similar problem exists in the missionary program among such minorities in the United States as American Indians and Mexican Americans. Should Mormons try to Americanize and Anglicize Indian and Mexican-American converts by integrating them rapidly with Anglo-American wards and branches? Or should they endeavor to insert Mormonism into their cultures and then try to strengthen local languages and cultures through independent wards and branches?

Anglo-American Mormons for the most part tend to share the typical Anglo-American contempt for the local Indian and Spanish languages and for the Indian and Mexican-American cultures. They usually agree with those Americans who argue that every effort should be made to persuade or to compel Indians and Mexican Americans to give up their native languages and cultures and become absorbed into the general American population--the melting pot concept.[8]

On the other hand, many American Indian and Mexican-American groups are struggling against this concept. They are convinced that they pay too high a price psychologically and as a group by Anglicizing and abandoning the culture and language of their people. The psychic wound caused by Anglo-American pressures is very deep and results in damaged identities, in marginality both to the native culture and to Anglo-American culture, in the adoption of such pathological escape mechanisms as alcohol, drugs, and sexual promiscuity, and in poverty and social deprivation. They also are not at all sure that, even if they did Anglicize, the American Mormons in the Southwest would accept them fully.

It is very important that Mormons realize that both the American Indian and Mexican-American peoples are acquiring a new sense of personal and cultural worth. They have become increasingly disenchanted with Anglo-American culture. Watergate; the spread of the hippie movement with its focus on drugs, alcohol, sexual promiscuity, and doing your own thing; the continued breakdown of the Anglo-American family; and other

indicators of social pathology are evidence to minority groups
that Anglo-American culture may be disintegrating. They are
beginning to reassess their own cultural values and have decided that many of these are superior to Anglo-American values.
As a result, they are no longer so interested in entering the
mainstream of American culture, but feel that they would be
psychologically, socially, culturally, and emotionally better
off if they developed the rich resources of their own native
languages and cultures. This does not mean that they do not
want to learn English, to improve their educational skills, or
to integrate politically and economically with other American
groups. They do, but they intend to remain Indian or Mexican
American and to assert their own cultural identity. They are
demanding that the Anglo-Americans accept and respect their
right to remain culturally different.
    The reemergence of once submerged local ethnic and minority
cultures is a worldwide phenomenon taking place in many large
nations. Canada, China, India, Pakistan, Burma, England,
Indonesia, Belgium, Germany, Russia, Brazil, and Mexico are
examples of nations facing serious problems caused by the rise
of ethnic consciousness and the assertion of ethnic identity
against the national identity of the dominant political, cultural, and social population elements. Glazer and Moynihan
state that in the United States they are "surprised at the
persistence and salience of ethnic-based forms of social identification and conflict."[9] They believe that ethnic identity,
ethnic assertion, and resultant social conflicts are increasing everywhere.
    Unfortunately many Mormons are either unaware of the grow-
ing strength among Mexican Americans and American Indians of
the movement to preserve their own culture, language, and
ethnic identities, or are hostile to it. The once strong movement of many Mexican-American and American Indian leaders
toward acculturation into and absorption by Anglo-American
society has about died. This very significant change in minority attitudes toward the melting-pot philosophy so popular
among Anglo-Americans has not yet won approval or acceptance.
Many southwestern Mormons have been in favor of closing out
missionary work in the Spanish language in much of the Spanish-
speaking Southwest. Mexican-American wards and branches have
been closed and their members amalgamated with Anglo-American,
English-speaking wards and branches. The results have been
tragic. Many Mexican Americans, not understanding English very
well or preferring to hear the gospel preached in Spanish, have
become inactive. Sadly, some of the best-educated Mexican-
American young people in the Church have drifted away into inactivity or hostility toward the Church. In certain areas, as
in the El Paso Stake, Mexican-American ward leaders, deeply

influenced by these new trends toward an assertion of a cultural identity, have come into conflict with a conservative Anglo-American stake leadership not aware of changing intellectual and emotional currents among the Mexican-American church members. This has created polarization between Mexican Americans and Anglo-Americans and has led to the disfellowshipping of some of the best educated and most faithful Mexican-American members of the Church. It is only a matter of time before the discontent of many Mexican-American Mormons leaks over into northern Mexico and harms the enormous progress of the Church there.

Missionary work among the American Indians and Mexican Americans has reached a crossroads. Other Christian churches are losing ground among them because of their failure to adjust to the rapidly changing currents of ethnic and cultural assertion and pride among Mexican Americans and American Indians. Mormonism may well suffer the same fate unless the desire of many Mexican Americans and American Indians to preserve their native languages, cultures, and ethnic identity is respected and incorporated into Mormon missionary activities.

The apparent Mormon slowness in making these adjustments among the Mexican Americans and American Indians is rather puzzling. In Polynesia, Mormonism more than any other Christian denomination has succeeded in incorporating its values and beliefs into the native Polynesian cultures. In the Pacific Islands, Mormonism has and is playing a most important role in preserving the physical identity of the Polynesian people, in strengthening and preserving their cultures against the intruding American and European cultures. The result is that in many Pacific islands Mormonism is no longer defined as something totally foreign, something white, something American, but as a national component of Polynesian cultures. Why cannot this successful model of missionary work be adapted and utilized in other areas and among other peoples, not only outside the United States but in missionary work among the American Indians and Mexican Americans? We are already training missionaries to work in the Navajo language. Can other Indian languages be used and can Mormonism be incorporated into native Indian and Mexican-American cultures so that it actually strengthens and indeed invigorates Indian cultures and languages? If this is not done, more and more American Indian and Mexican-American leaders may come to view Mormonism as but another Anglo-American social and religious system, an obstacle in their march toward full cultural and linguistic autonomy and equality in the United States.[10]

Now to return once more to the Anglo-American Mormon community. An intriguing question that fairly cries for research is whether or not diverse Mormon subcultures have come into existence within the basic Mormon core area of southern Idaho, Utah, and Arizona. Do both urban and rural Mormons in this vast region share the same life styles, personal aspirations, religious and secular beliefs and values, and behavior patterns? Or have regional and urban-rural differences emerged? Or did such differences once exist in the past, but now have been papered over by mass media, urbanization, and similar educational and church systems?

At the present time Mormons are predominantly an urban community. The old claim once made that urbanization would severely weaken if not destroy the Mormon value system and religious practices has been answered in the negative. Distinctive rapidly growing Mormon urban groupings are emerging in most of the larger American metropolitan centers. The Mormon population of these urban nuclei is drawn from diverse sources ranging from immigrants from the Mormon core region in the Rocky Mountains and California to local converts. Again the interesting question comes up for answer: Are these diverse Mormon population clusters forming distinctive local cultural and religious characteristics that to some degree may differentiate them from their fellow Mormons in other metropolitan centers?[11] I am personally persuaded that there is some evidence that this is happening. Living for a long period of time in a metropolitan center with a fairly large Mormon population drawn from diverse sources, I encountered the following: Mormon immigrants from the English-speaking Mormon colonies in Mexico were thought to be the most orthodox in religion and the most conservative in political behavior. Indeed they at times were thought by other Mormons to have an old-fashioned aura about them. Utah Mormons had the reputation of taking their Mormonism for granted and of being a bit lackadaisical in their religious obligations. California Mormons, on the other hand, were defined as being more liberal politically than other Mormons and more worldly and sophisticated in behavior. One wonders what might be said about the Mormon communities in, say, Berkeley, California; Cambridge, Massachusetts; New York City; Chicago; Miami; or Portland, Oregon.

Mormon and non-Mormon relationships in Utah as well as elsewhere have always fascinated the observer. It is rather unfortunate that in spite of the growing number of excellent Mormon historians and social scientists so few objective or detailed analytical studies of this ever-interesting human area of social interaction and accommodation exist. Such studies could well begin with the social, economic, and political dimensions of the bitter, chaotic, multi-faceted struggles between Mormon and non-Mormon groups in the state in the late nineteenth and early twentieth centuries. It seems apparent that the basic economic, political, and social variables

responsible for the conflicts have been masked by apparent
religious and moral overtones. It is also unfortunate that
we do not as yet possess a series of decent biographical studies of the major Mormon, non-Mormon, and apostate Mormon individuals involved in these conflicts. Not even among such a
history-conscious people as the Mormons are there many scholarly, objective biographies of the Mormon giants of the time.

Scholarly light could also be cast upon the complicated
and obscure maneuvers involved in accommodating local and national non-Mormon and Mormon political, economic, social, and
religious interests, in shaping the compromises and truces that
ended overt Mormon and non-Mormon hostilities in order that
Utah could become a state. One senses from reading the newspapers of the times and from stories related within families
that complicated discussions and maneuverings went on behind
the scenes between Mormon and non-Mormon local and national
political and business leaders. What pressures were exerted
by whom upon local Mormons and non-Mormons to bring about an
acceptable compromise are not fully known. Who were the go-
betweens and what were the offers and counter-offers presented
as part of the bargaining procedures before acceptable compromises were hammered out?

The formation of class structures--or what is known among
sociologists as the process of social stratification--is another
related issue in Utah that still remains shrouded in scholarly
darkness. As the non-Mormon population in Utah expanded, one
senses that two segregated class systems came into existence,
one Mormon and the other non-Mormon, with little friendly social interaction between them. As conflicts intensified between the two groups, their social isolation from each other
may have increased. Go-betweens certainly existed; jack
Mormons and non-Mormons friendly to Mormon leaders maintained
the essential communication between the two groups. We have
very little information about the Mormon and non-Mormon societies before the end of the century or about the networks of
communication and mediation between them.

As the realization spread among both Mormons and non-Mormons that economic and political development were hampered by
ongoing conflicts, efforts were made by certain elements in
both communities to accommodate their differences. Civic and
private clubs came into existence accepting both Mormons and
non-Mormons as members, and soon Mormons and non-Mormons were
interacting with each other on more complex personal, social,
economic, and political levels than ever before. But it is
not known whether or not two parallel social structures, Mormon and non-Mormon, exist in Utah with communication between
them carried out by networks of jack Mormons and non-Mormons
friendly to Mormon and non-Mormon interests alike or whether

Mormon and non-Mormon social-class, business, and professional groupings have by now merged into a single stratified social structure. Only research can provide us with sufficient data to clarify the issue.

The internal socioeconomic characteristics of the Mormon class structure are also poorly understood. Two contrasting assumptions can be made. One is that Mormon values, Mormon identity, and Mormon religious activities are still strong enough to contain incipient social class formation and resultant social strain. If this is true, then the Mormon skilled, semi-skilled, and unskilled workers should be as loyal to Mormon values and as active in Mormon church organizations as Mormon professional, white collar, and managerial elements. The other assumption is that the Mormon community today is becoming largely middle class, and that Mormon working-class members are not as active in Mormon organizations and activities as before, because of a sense of social alienation. The two assumptions could be tested by exploring the differential levels of religious identity and activity of diverse socioeconomic strata within the urban Mormon communities of Utah. Similar data could be secured by comparing Mormon and non-Mormon union members in regards to union loyalty and attitude toward union leadership. That is, which are more responsive, Mormon or non-Mormon union members? Which are more loyal to their unions? If, by any chance, Mormon and union leaders should adopt conflicting policies on economic issues, to which set of loyalties, union or Mormon, would Mormon workers respond first?

Residential segregation is another aspect of Mormon and non-Mormon accommodation that is worth exploring. I was informed by a real estate salesman in Salt Lake City recently that many real estate salesmen show homes to non-Mormons in neighborhoods with large existing non-Mormon populations and tend to avoid neighborhoods that are predominantly Mormon. A casual investigation of my own neighborhood in Salt Lake City revealed some clustering of non-Mormon home owners. That is, they were not randomly distributed through the neighborhood.

Related to the question of segregation is the formation of central zones of urban decay, marked by associated urban problems of poverty, crime, juvenile delinquency, and other types of urban pathology common to American cities everywhere. These central zones are increasingly inhabited by poor people and by members of minorities. The origin of the urban poor in Salt Lake City and Ogden is a source of some debate among interested circles. Some claim that the majority of the white urban poor in Utah are native-born Utahns, primarily Mormon, who migrated from rural Mormon communities in the 1930s and 1940s in search of urban employment and were caught in poverty.

Others claim that the majority of the urban white poor are migrants from other states who came to Utah in search of employment since the 1930s or after. Except for data provided by the U.S. Census Bureau little is known about the origin or the socioeconomic characteristics of low-income white inhabitants of the urban zones of poverty in Utah.

The cultural and social influences that Mormon and non-Mormon communities exert upon each other is an interesting field of scholarly endeavor that has not been explored. Mormon religious and cultural pressures upon non-Mormons through neighborhood associations, missionary endeavors, and the attraction of Mormon child and youth activities are rather heavy. Undoubtedly Mormon values do influence in many subtle and not so subtle ways the social life, the values, and the attitudes of non-Mormons. A considerable percentage of non-Mormons join the Mormon Church as a result of these pressures. Other non-Mormons may develop a heightened sense of their own religious identity as Protestants, Jews, and Catholics and may be led into greater religious activity and identification than they might have had outside of Utah where such pressures as those exerted by Mormonism are absent. And, of course, many non-Mormons become quite hostile and embittered toward the Mormons because of the social pressures that they experience.

Undoubtedly Mormon values infiltrate non-Mormon religious and secular organizations. A non-Mormon friend coming to Utah stated that he was quite surprised at the degree to which Protestants and Catholics in Salt Lake City had acquired Mormon values without recognizing the fact. Part of this infiltration comes from dissident Mormons who have joined other religious denominations and part comes undoubtedly from the subconscious process of daily interaction with Mormons and from Mormon mass media.

The accommodative process of immigrant adjustment in Utah is another area of accommodation that is just now receiving considerable scholarly attention. But most of this attention has been devoted to non-Mormon Italian and slavic immigrants coming to Utah in the late nineteenth and early twentieth centuries.[12] The American West Center at the University of Utah has become a focus of such studies. But it is not often recognized that the urban communities of Utah have also received substantial immigration of Mormon converts from Europe and from the Middle East since World War II. Many of them have organized their own wards and branches. Very little is known about their coming, their socioeconomic characteristics, their patterns of settlement, the degree to which they retain their native cultures and languages, and the problems of adjustment to Utah.[13]

Turning now to the accommodative process involving Utah social minorities, we shall make a few comments about American Indians, blacks, Mexican Americans, and Asians. We begin with the American Indians, since they are the poorest, most neglected, and perhaps the most exploited minority group, not only in Utah but in the United States. Although Brigham Young adopted the policy of feeding the Indians rather than fighting them, the Utah Indians were still dispossessed of their lands by Mormons. The process of land alienation from the Indians was perhaps a bit smoother, with less violence than elsewhere, but the end result was still the same. The Indians lost their lands and autonomy, and control of their own lives. It is significant that those Indian tribes that suffered the most in Utah, the Utes and the Shoshones, are still quite resistant to Mormon missionary endeavors. On the other hand, tribes such as the Navajo and other southwestern tribes that were only indirectly affected by Mormon settlement policies view the Mormons far more favorably. One aspect of the accommodation process seldom mentioned by students of either Mormon or Utah history is that some intermarriage between Mormon settlers and Indian women took place. A certain amount of Ute, Shoshone, and Paiute genes crept into the modern Mormon genetic heritage. A study of these mixed marriages would be interesting.

To a considerable degree the Utes, Shoshones, and Paiutes have not recovered psychologically, culturally, or socially from the traumatic and tragic impact of the unjust treatment received at the hands of Utah whites. On the other hand, the Navajos, with their large reservation, their preservation of their culture and language, had little intimate white contact until the 1930s. They enjoyed what might be sardonically called a policy of "benign neglect." Their reservation has aptly been described as "islands of uranium floating on a sea of oil," and the Navajo reservation cannot support its rapidly growing population. Thousands of Navajos are forced to migrate off the reservation in search of employment. Many are entering the agricultural migrant labor stream at a time when the stream is beginning to dry up because of the mechanization of agriculture. Unless both federal and state governments develop programs to provide employment and teach vocational skills to the Navajo, we may have some serious problems in the future. More and more Navajos in Utah and elsewhere are moving to town.[14]

Although some Indian tribal governments in Utah are trying to develop the recreational potential of their reservations with the assistance of public and private agencies, the Indians in Utah have not been very active in either the political or the cultural life of Utah. It is predictable that as Indians become politically active they will run Indian candidates for local and state office. This means that serious conflicts may develop between Indian political organizations and local white groups that may feel threatened by rising Indian political activities.

Local political parties in Utah could minimize potential Indian-white conflict by paying far more attention now and in the future than they have in the past to Indian needs and aspirations. They ought to be thinking about registering Indian voters and educating them about the purposes and mechanics of the American political system and about the formation of party organizations on Indian reservations. They should also place on their tickets qualified Indian candidates acceptable to the local Indian population. Even though such a development would be attacked by more militant Indian leaders as a process of cooption and weakening of Indian political strength, it might well prevent the rise of Indian-white hostility in the counties containing substantial Indian populations. The incorporation of the Utah Indian into the political life of the state is after all but part of the same democratic process that witnessed the incorporation of the European immigrant and more recently the American black into the American political process.

Not only are Utah Indians coming into the larger urban centers of Utah, but they are also joined there by Indians from all parts of the United States. The movement, a very reluctant movement, of Indians in the United States from the rural areas to the urban areas is accelerating. Indian urban population is growing. Most Indians in the United States today do not live on reservations or have reservations to fall back on.

Although the American West Center at the University of Utah has initiated studies of urban Indians in Salt Lake City and is assisting Indian tribes to write their own tribal history, much more needs to be done. I certainly would like to encourage scholars at Brigham Young University, the school with the largest number of Indian students in the West, to study the problems and characteristics of the urbanizing Indian and also to develop programs to help Indians overcome the problems of urban adjustment.

If all the Indians in Utah were to vote as a block, they could dominate close statewide elections in Utah as they could also in Arizona, New Mexico, and Oklahoma. I suspect that all of us are in for some surprises in the future, as the Indians begin to flex their burgeoning political and economic muscles. The fundamental issue is this: Can we accept the Indian's right to maintain his culture, language, and tribal identity, and assist him to expand his landholdings and to overcome the deadly problems of disease, poverty, and damaged identity, and finally accept him on the basis of complete equality as an American who dares to be different?

From the time of the early Mormon pioneers, Utah has been home to a persistent black community concentrated along the Wasatch Front. The descendants of these black pioneers have been joined by recurrent waves of black migrants, beginning with the use of blacks as railroad porters and workers in the early twentieth century. Each major war has seen blacks recruited to meet Utah labor needs. Since the end of World War II, other blacks have migrated to Utah as workers in federal agencies, as students at the various state universities, and as employees of the larger corporations. As a result, Utah blacks form a diverse but distinctive black community with cultural and socioeconomic characteristics somewhat different from those of black communities in other parts of the United States. Among these differences is the existence of a small black Mormon group that lies submerged within a larger black community. Unfortunately again, the black community in this state has received very little scholarly attention.[15]

The largest minority in Utah, the Mexican Americans, are a remarkably heterogeneous people. Among them exist many quite diverse subgroupings. The largest Mexican-American subgrouping in Utah came from northern New Mexico and southern Colorado. Spanish-speaking people from this region entered Utah as Indian traders and hunters long before the Mormons settled in Salt Lake Valley. They have continued to come in substantial numbers ever since, as sheep herders, miners, defense workers, farmers, and government employees. Since the turn of the century they have been joined by numerous Mexican Americans from the lower Rio Grande Valley of Texas who enter the state every year to harvest many farm crops. Around two or three hundred families settle out of the migrant stream every year in Utah. And finally many legal and illegal Mexican immigrants come to Utah directly from Mexico. Concentrated primarily along the Wasatch Front, Mexican-American communities also exist in mining towns, farming communities, and sheep ranching areas throughout Utah.[16]

Another important minority group is now defined as the Asians. The Chinese were probably the first Asians of record to arrive in Utah, coming as railroad workers when the railroad penetrated the state from the west. Many dropped out of railroad employment to open laundries, restaurants, and other retail businesses. At one time Chinatowns existed in a number of Utah communities. By now almost all of them have vanished, although a small number of Chinese merchants and their families live in almost all of the larger towns in the state.

The Japanese Americans were the next to arrive. They also came into the state as railroad workers and miners. Gradually they moved out of mining and railroad employment and pioneered in the development of intensive commercial vegetable farming in Utah. Many are still found farming, but the majority by now have left agriculture for various professional and commercial pursuits. A small number of Japanese entered Utah as wives of Utah servicemen stationed in Japan. Small circles of racially intermarried couples came into existence in the larger Utah communities. Very little is known about these families, their social acceptance, the cultural and psychological problems that they encountered, or the degree of marital success or failure that they have experienced.

The American Japanese, the American Chinese, and the smaller numbers of Koreans and other Asian groupings that have entered Utah have for the most part escaped the scrutiny of social scientists. The pioneer work of Dr. Elmer Smith of the Department of Anthropology at the University of Utah in the study of the American Japanese resident in Utah during the 1930s has never been followed up.[17] The Asians are considered by students of racial minorities to be quite a success story, having encountered and overcome significant obstacles, but the contributions of the American Chinese and American Japanese to the economic growth and development of Utah have been overlooked.

Virtually all of these minority groups in the United States, including Utah, have been stirred by conflicting political, economic, and social currents. It is rather significant that Utah escaped the minority violence that troubled the United States in the 1960s. This fortunate situation came about for many reasons, and they need exploring by social scientists. It may be that the economic and social problems and discrimination encountered in Utah are not as harsh for minorities as they are in other sections of the country. It may be that minority leaders in Utah were able to exert better social control over their own people than similar leaders in other parts of the country. Or the fact that Utah has no large segregated ghettos or *barrios*, as Mexican-American neighborhoods are called. Members of most minorities live in poverty-stricken but integrated neighborhoods. At any rate, the fact that Utah did escape minority violence, although not minority unrest, is worthy of exploration for what it may tell us about the accommodative processes involving minority groups in Utah, and for the insights that such studies may provide us about the dominant ethnic and religious groupings in Utah, the nature of the local political process, the communication networks between minority organizations, and the political and economic leadership of the state.

Although the militant minority organizations, leaders, and programs of the 1960s have ebbed, the fundamental problems of poverty, unemployment, discrimination, ill health, and inadequate housing still remain. Although enormous progress was certainly made in the 1960s to resolve these problems, it is still true that almost all the civil rights legislation passed during this period did little to help the majority of poor minority members to secure better housing, employment, health services, nutrition, and neighborhood environments. Massive minority poverty still remains unsolved. It is inevitable that in time a new generation of minority group leaders will replace the older ones who are passing off the scene. It is inevitable that protest organizations will be formed and pressure once again exerted against the national society to ameliorate the socioeconomic conditions in which minority groups live. It would therefore behoove all of us in the present period of relative quiet and peace to struggle to resolve these problems, which to some degree are a socioeconomic abscess eating away at the health of our larger cities, before built-up minority pressures again force us to develop hurried programs.

In closing our discussion on minority groups, it might be observed that the minority groups in Utah are just now coming under scholarly scrutiny. The processes of accommodation between the various minority groups themselves and between the minorities and the dominant socioeconomic groups in Utah still remain to be studied. Attention is usually focused on the relationships between the minorities and the dominant group, and very little attention has been devoted to researching the diverse attitudes of minority groups toward other minority groups. Minority people may share the prejudices of the dominant socioeconomic groups toward other minorities and even toward their own minority. These attitudes do change. Thus at one time the lighter-skinned blacks were more highly valued and rated not only by whites but also by other blacks. To a major degree the "black is beautiful" and Black Power movements tried to free blacks from this crippling pathological downgrading of their own skin color and hair forms. Now the lighter-skinned blacks are apt to be discriminated against by the darker-skinned blacks as well as by the white society.

It is also interesting to note that because blacks were the first major minority group to engage in a determined multifaceted campaign to move into the mainstream of American society, they soon preempted the attention of many American businessmen and government officials not fully aware of the existence of other minority groups in the United States. Many blacks hired by government agencies were given positions of responsibility in programs providing services to nonblack minorities. Members of these minorities, if they became dissatisfied with the services rendered, attacked black administrators of programs as part of what they defined as the "oppressive establishment." This was rather an uncomfortable experience for black agency personnel who but a few years earlier were often using the same language to criticize the same agencies that now employed them.

Many white agency heads in Utah and elsewhere come under unexpected heavy fire when they employ blacks to administer programs concerned primarily with American Indians and Mexican Americans. Most minorities today want programs directed at them to be headed and staffed by their own people and are no more apt to accept administrators of other minority groups than they are to accept white administrators. It is always essential in order to understand the ever-changing, complex processes of accommodation among minority groups to assess the nature of such relationships between minority groups as well as between the minorities and the dominant society.

The situation in Utah is even more complex than it may be elsewhere. Many minority leaders in Utah familiar with the history of discrimination, persecution, and violence inflicted upon the Mormons by "white Anglo-Saxon Protestants," the "Wasps" against whom today's minorities are often struggling, tend to expect from Mormons a greater sympathy and support for their goals, aspirations, and social movements than they do from other Christian denominations and white organizations. At times disillusioned, they express their resentments through sharp attacks upon and criticisms of Mormons. In Utah this criticism may be muted at times, through informal negotiations and discussions with Mormon leaders that may lead to a quiet support of moderate minority demands and groups within the state. The uneasy, ever-changing process of accommodation between minorities and Mormons in Utah is a fascinating subject worthy of the attention of both Mormon and non-Mormon scholars.

Minority numbers are rather small in Utah. The socioeconomic situation, except for the American Indians, may be better than it is in other regions. Few historical memories of prolonged ethnic and racial conflicts or historic injustice exist to poison relationships--except, again, among the American Indians. Although considerable social and economic discrimination exists, little residential segregation can be found. It should therefore be easier to improve racial and ethnic relations in Utah than elsewhere unless existing situations change or new, charismatic, militant minority leaders emerge. In Utah, however, the minorities do not occupy the center of the stage; this position is still reserved for Mormon-to-non-Mormon relationships.

Out of the prolonged historic struggles between Mormons and non-Mormons in Utah a unique set of accommodative mechanisms, it seems, came into existence to prevent dangerous polarization, especially Mormon-non-Mormon polarization over political, economic, or social issues. Even those involved in resolving social problems or mediating group conflicts may not be fully aware of these mechanisms, or of the manner in which they function. At times the mechanisms may be confusing, baffling, or irritating to leaders of racial and ethnic groups, student groups, groups of poor people, and other groups; yet they seem to have been effective enough to maintain social peace in Utah. Of course there is no promise that they will be equally effective in the future. This is especially true when passions over issues run deep and polarity between social groups increases. Even then, however, they may still function. The existence of these accommodative mechanisms is one reason why in what has been so often defined as a rather conservative state, liberals are elected to office, the electorate may swing from a conservative to a liberal position, and compromises emerge that in some states might be defined as rather radical.

The first stage of these accommodative mechanisms comes into play when new social issues surface. The first tendency in Utah among many leaders is to deny that the issue exists or is very significant. This attitude antagonizes those who believe that the issue is an important one that at least deserves serious treatment. While this goes on, efforts are quietly made by state political, religious, and economic leaders to ascertain the seriousness of the issue, the amount of public support that the leaders pressing the issue may possess and their potential for polarity or for disturbance of the public tranquility. If the issue and those who raise it do not seem to have much public support and they clearly do not trouble any significant element in the state, then the state leaders may promptly forget about the issue or deny its significance. Those fighting for the issue may then have serious difficulties in attracting media attention or in placing their position before the public. They may come to feel that they are hitting at a feather pillow. The feathers fly but nothing happens.

If the leaders of the state come to believe that the problem is serious, that many people are involved, and that it could lead to confrontations dangerous to social unity, then efforts will be made by the state leaders to find a compromise acceptable to them. They may offer half a loaf to the other side. At this stage, a mutual tug-of-war goes on, each side trying to assess the other side's strength, determination, and negotiating skills. Dependent on these mutual assessments, a compromise is eventually hammered out that sometimes results in some very curious legislation. The on-going low-key controversy over "liquor by the drink" is an excellent example of the way that such issues are resolved. No one is really satisfied, but parties to the dispute are satisfied enough not to continue the conflict.

A smart leader in this situation is one who learns how to manipulate the mass media in order to keep his cause before the public and who can create the impression that the issue is an important one worthy of attention and that, unless it is resolved to the satisfaction of the group involved, serious problems may develop in the future. The greatest mistake that this leader can make is to bluster, threaten, be violent in language or in behavior, neglect the rules of courtesy in public discourse, or create violent confrontations. If he is rather low key but firm, willing to engage in private discussion of issues, and gives the impression of being a reasonable man in search of mutually satisfying rational solutions or compromises, he may have considerable influence.

The advantages of these accommodative social mechanisms are evident. Utah managed to escape the violent eruptions that troubled American cities and universities during the 1960s and early 1970s. Although militant racial and ethnic leaders have been active in Utah, they have seldom been able to function effectively and have either left the state or modified their tactics. Social conflicts have been adjusted and compromises developed. Human needs to some degree have been met and unrest kept to a viable level.

Another example that might be cited of a current issue undergoing this same social and political process is land use planning legislation. Land erosion on livestock ranges and mountains, canyon developments that threaten purity of water supplies and wildlife habitat, and the massive spread of poorly planned housing and recreational developments all impose heavy financial and social costs upon society and increasingly upon the individual taxpayer. A few informed citizens have tried to arouse public concern, but without major success in Utah. Until a larger number of Utah citizens personally suffer from uncontrolled land use, they are apt to listen to the blandishments of those who proclaim the right of every property owner to use his property as he desires regardless of the harmful impact of improper land use upon other people.

The leaders of the movement in favor of some constraints upon unrestricted land use managed to persuade members of the state legislature of both political parties to pass a rather mild and weak bill. Immediately conservative groups, appealing to an electorate not fully awakened to the problems of uncontrolled land use, managed to defeat the measure in a state referendum. As with the housing problem, unless federal legislation is passed, many years may now elapse before effective land use planning evolves. Land use legislation will not be reconsidered until the public demands it. By then, the costs of resolving the problems of uncontrolled land use will undoubtedly be very much greater and the problem far more difficult to solve than they are now.

However, the social costs of these accommodative mechanisms have also been serious. The process in Utah of resolving issues and developing compromises is a very slow and cumbersome one. It is at times difficult for far-seeing men, aware of developing realities that may not seem important at the time but that will become important at a later period, to secure an audience or to have the issue resolved before it does become a serious social problem. Several times in Utah history issues have come to the attention of public leaders that were ignored until significant elements in the population had come to press them. Issues that might have been resolved at low economic and social costs are often not dealt with in Utah until a time when they can no longer be ignored, and then must be resolved at far higher social and economic costs.

Public housing is an excellent example. Federal legislation establishing public housing programs in the United States came into existence in the 1930s. Utah was one of the few states that did not take advantage of these programs until very recently. Many men had pointed out the need for public housing programs in the larger metropolitan centers of the state from the 1950s on, but little attention was given to them by community leaders or by the public at large. As these men in favor of public housing seemed to have little following or political strength, they were virtually ignored. Conservative groups not in favor of such programs were able through constant agitation to prevent their adoption for many years. It was not until the problem became so serious that it actually seemed to threaten the future of such cities as Salt Lake City that conservative opposition died away and the state legislature and city and county governments of Salt Lake finally adopted housing programs. By this time, housing costs had risen so high and federal support had diminished so greatly that it had become extremely costly to develop an adequate public housing program. Now the state of Utah and the city and county of Salt Lake will inevitably have to pay far more than they would have had to if housing programs had been adopted ten or twenty years earlier.

As old issues are resolved or pushed into the background unresolved, new issues constantly rise to trouble the public mind. The most significant of these new issues, apparently, is the question of energy development. It seems as though the political and economic leaders of the state are determined to press for the development of these resources as quickly as possible because of the potential increase in public tax revenue and the economic development of static or declining rural counties. A basic truism is in danger of being forgotten. Economic development always benefits some human groups to the detriment of other human groups. Some groups benefit and some must pay the costs. The two are not always the same.

Thus in a semiarid state such as Utah it seems wise to raise the question of where the large amounts of water needed for energy development are coming from. If all water rights in the state have been allocated, what groups will lose their water? Is it wise to allocate such enormous amounts of water to a single industry, or should water be reserved for other uses? Undoubtedly the economic development of other communities or of future industries may be sharply limited or handicapped by the allocation of water to energy development. Another question is the possibility of Utah becoming in essence a colony, a provider of power to California and Arizona. Decisions about power allocation or power use in these states may threaten the economic prosperity of several counties in Utah without their being able to influence the decisions that affect their future. Apparently California and Arizona will get the benefit of additional energy. Will the tax revenues and the jobs provided outweigh the costs of the water provided, the public services such as roads and schools, the air and water pollution, and other similar social costs? Somewhere along the line, someone ought to draw up a simple balance sheet of benefits and costs and strike a balance while there is still time to do so.

In terminating our discussion of the processes of accommodation in Utah time has not permitted us to dwell upon many areas, such as the urbanization of the state, the decline of the small farmer, the gradual diminishing of jobs for migrant farm workers caused by mechanization of agriculture, the complex role of social and civic clubs and organizations in bringing Mormons and non-Mormons together, the rise of the labor union, and the ever-corrosive impact of secularization upon the people of Utah. But I hope that at least I have given you an idea not only of the insight but also the knowledge about ourselves and our society that a study of the processes of accommodation can provide us.

REFERENCES

1. Alvin L. Bertrand, Basic Sociology (New York: Appelton-Century-Crofts, 1967), pp. 212-17. See also Mavis Biesanz and John Biesanz, Introduction to Sociology (Englewood Cliffs, N.J., 1969), pp. 114-17.

2. Ibid.

3. Ibid.

4. Michael Novak, The Rise of the Unmeltable Ethnics (New York: The Macmillan Publishing Co., 1973), p. 376.

5. F. La Mond Tullis, in "Politics and Society: Anglo American Mormonism in a Revolutionary Land," BYU Studies, 13(Winter 1973):126-34; and Wesley W. Craig, Jr., in "The Church in Latin America: Progress and Challenge," Dialogue: A Journal of Mormon Thought, 5(Autumn 1970):79-86, make essentially the same observations.

6. F. La Mond Tullis, in "Three Myths about Mormons in Latin America" (Dialogue, Spring 1972), thoughtfully discusses the social and economic problems faced by Latin Americans who join the Church. His conclusions undoubtedly apply to other areas in the world where Mormonism is reaching out toward peoples who live in poverty and possess cultures quite different from the culture of Anglo-American Mormons.

7. The rapidly growing Mormon community in Mexico should provide a good opportunity to analyze the class structure within the Mormon community as well as the differential social and economic pressures applied to Mormons by non-Mormons in diverse class settings. In 1968 I was part of a team that studied three Protestant groups in Juarez, Mexico: the Assembly of God, the Methodists, and the Baptists. Our findings indicated that members of these groups moving into the Mexican middle- and upper-class groupings faced increased economic and social pressures that led many of them to join the Roman Catholic Church. Apparently the pressures of Catholicism are stronger in these social settings than among poorer Mexican groups. Mexico is such a diverse country that our findings may be relevant for Juarez but not for other Mexican cities.

8. The following is a quote from a 1967 letter from Donald E. Matthews, mission president at San Antonio, to Leo Grebler, Joan W. Moore, and Ralph C. Guzman, the authors of The Mexican American People (New York: The Free Press, 1970):

> Initially in each area a separate church is established (for the Mexican Americans), for the principal reason of teaching these people in their own tongue. Within the same area, English speaking churches are established and these people are free to go to whichever they choose, and then ultimately there is a consolidation and in these churches English is the language which is spoken. . . . The policy of the Church over the years, throughout

> its history, has been that English is the
> language of this country and that as fast
> as people can learn the language there
> need not be any separation between them
> and other members of the Church (p. 507).

This still seems to be the existing policy. The authors of the book cited state:

> Thus the Mormon Church body is theologically conservative, with a special niche for the Mexican Americans that seems to exaggerate the patronizing tendencies implicit in other evangelizing Protestant sects and denominations. But its rigorous adherence to certain norms of procedure seems more effective in attaining the objectives to "Americanize through evangelization" than the policies of denominations which in the past made this an explicit goal" (p. 507).

It is this policy of Americanization through evangelization that offends more and more Mexican Americans and is creating a growing tension between the Mormon Church and large numbers of Mexican-American Mormons as well as non-Mormons.

9. Nathan Glazer and Daniel P. Moynihan, "Why Ethnicity," Commentary, 58(October 1974):33-39.

10. Discussion based on conversations with returned missionaries and immigrants from Polynesia.

11. Armand L. Mauss, in two articles, "Moderation in All Things: Political and Social Outlooks of Modern Urban Mormons," Dialogue, 7(Spring 1972); and "Saints, Cities, and Secularism: Religious Attitudes and Behavior of Modern Urban Mormons," Dialogue, 7(Summer 1972):8-27, argues that his studies indicate some differences in values and attitudes between Utah and California urban Mormons.

12. See Helen Z. Papanikolas, "Toil and Rage in a New Land: The Greek Immigrants in Utah," in an entire issue of the Utah Historical Quarterly devoted to Greek Immigrants to Utah, Utah Historical Quarterly, 38(Spring 1970):373-92; "Utah's Coal Lands: A Vital Example of How America Became a Great Nation," Utah Historical Quarterly, 43(Spring 1975):102-24; Joseph Stipanovich, "South Slave Settlements in Utah, 1890-1935," Utah

Historical Quarterly, 43(Spring 1975):155-63; and Philip F. Notarianni, "Italian Fraternal Organizations in Utah, 1897-1934," Utah Historical Quarterly, 43(Spring 1975):172-87.

13. A few studies on Mormon immigrant groups: William Mulder, Homeward to Zion: The Mormon Migration from Scandinavia (Minneapolis: University of Minnesota Press, 1957), 225 pp.; P. H. M. Taylor, "Why Did British Mormons Emigrate," Utah Historical Quarterly, 24(July 1956):195-214; Thomas L. Broadbent, "The Salt Lake City Beobachter: Mirror of an Immigration," Utah Historical Quarterly, 25(July 1957):329-50; Douglas A. Alder, "The German Speaking Immigration to Utah from 1850-1950," Master's thesis, University of Utah, 1959; and Kate B. Carter, ed., "Contributions of the Icelanders," Heart Throbs of the West, 2(Salt Lake City, 1940):295-300.

14. Although no comprehensive studies of resident Indian groups in Utah have been made, a number of articles do exist, among them the following: Richard O. Ulibarri, "Utah's Ethnic Minorities," Utah Historical Quarterly, 40(Summer 1972):pp. 210-32 (he also treats other Utah minorities in this article, including blacks, Asians, and Mexicans); Coulson and Geneva Wright, "Indian-White Relations in the Uintah Basin," Utah Humanities Review, 2(October 1948):319-45; Omer C. Stewart, "Ute Indians: Before and after White Contact," Utah Historical Quarterly, 34(Winter 1966):36-61; Floyd A. O'Neil, "An Anguished Odyssey: The Flight of the Utes, 1906-1908," Utah Historical Quarterly, 36(Fall 1968):315-27; an entire issue of the Utah Historical Quarterly, 39(Spring 1971), devoted to the Utah Indians with one article on the Hopis; articles written by Catherine S. and Don D. Fowler, Robert W. Delaney, and Henry Harris, Jr.; and interviews with Floyd O'Neil, J. Lee Correll, James B. Allen, and Ted J. Warner, Charles S. Peterson, and Ergrude Chapoose Willie, interviewed by Norma Denver.

15. Among the studies of Utah blacks that have been made are the following: Dennis L. Lythgoe, "Negro Slavery in Utah," Utah Historical Quarterly, 39(Winter 1971):40-54; and Kate B. Carter, The Story of the Negro Pioneer (Salt Lake City, 1965), 39 pp.

16. Jerald H. Merrill, "Fifty Years with a Future: Salt Lake's Guadalupe Mission and Parish," Utah Historical Quarterly, 40(Summer 1972):242-64. See also E. Ferol Benavides, "The Saints among the Saints: A Study of Curanderismo in Utah," Utah Historical Quarterly, 39(Autumn 1973):373-92; Vincent Mayer, "Oral History: Another Approach to Ethnic History," pp. 1-5; Paul Morgan and Vincent Mayer, "The Spanish-Speaking

Population of Utah: From 1900 to 1935," p. 62; Ann Nelson, "Spanish-Speaking Migrant Laborers in Utah, 1950 to 1965," pp. 63-111; and Greg Coranado, "Spanish Speaking Organizations in Utah," pp. 112-27--all found in <u>Toward a History of the Spanish-Speaking People of Utah</u>, American West Center, University of Utah, 1973.

Comparative Frontiers:
China and the West
Paul V. Hyer

> Historians have long been concerned about the transferability of generalizations made about one frontier condition--particularly the American--to other frontiers. In this essay, Paul V. Hyer, professor of history at Brigham Young University, has contrasted the condition of the nineteenth-century Chinese frontier in Mongolia with that of the American and to some extent the Russian frontiers.
> The comparisons provide some interesting contrasts. Where the image of the American frontier was generally favorable and positive, the Mongol frontier was bleak. Historians in the United States following Frederick Jackson Turner have seen the American frontier as contributing a great deal to the development of significant aspects of the American character. In Mongolia, by contrast, the frontier apparently had little impact on the character of the Chinese who moved into the area. Like the American frontier, however, both private individuals and governmental representatives became promoters of land development and other schemes. Thus, if Hyer's insights have any applicability to frontier development, it may well be that the common denominator of the frontier situation is avarice rather than democracy.

Most frontier studies in Western languages are concerned with the phenomena of Caucasian peoples moving into the lands of non-Caucasian peoples, notable cases being the American West and Russia's Siberian frontier. Other studies, treating frontier situations in such places as Africa, Latin America, Australia, and Canada, concern mainly European colonization. It is not generally realized that the Chinese are one of the great pioneering peoples of world history. Expanding from the cradle of the Yellow River to cover the great area of China, their frontier experience extends over thousands of years of contact, especially with Altaic nomadic peoples.

One characteristic of frontiers wherever they may be is that dominant, expanding societies generally take an unenlightened, if not brutal, attitude towards their frontier minority problems. Best known is the superior attitude of white Americans towards minority frontier peoples, echoing the condescending attitude of Europeans towards "natives" contacted during the period of expansion. This can also be seen in the strong historical sense of sinocentrism (ta-Han chu-i) which has led Chinese to either ignore "barbarian" frontier nationalities or to force their assimilation. It has been particularly difficult for so-called sophisticated peoples to give sympathetic treatment to the culture and historical development of frontier peoples. This approach seems to be changing and, while it may be a premature judgment, it appears that a growing universal social consciousness is awakening people in both the East and the West to a closer study of the past history and present problems of frontier peoples.

Of particular concern here is the comparatively recent movement of Chinese beyond the Great Wall into Mongol lands—an important case of one Asian people's colonization and displacement of a neighboring Asian nationality. The modern Mongol frontier has attracted many military men and merchants, some anthropologists and missionaries, but few historians. Recently a few scholars have been studying frontier railroad development, and some work is being done on Chinese migration, the Russian threat, and diplomatic developments with regard to China's northern frontier. A great deal of study yet remains to be done, not only on the Chinese movement outward creating a frontier, but also on the other side, the story of the Mongolian nomads. Their tragic experience on the China frontier cries for attention.

A standard definition of a frontier is the border or confines of a country abutting on the territory of another, or the part of a country furthest advanced or nearest to an unsettled or uncivilized region. At least part of this definition would be contested by native peoples who would reject the expanding society's biased notion as to what constitutes civilization. But this is a rather academic matter. A much more practical problem has been the challenge to the use of the land by the indigenous people on both the American and Asian frontiers.

The China-Mongol frontier, like most frontiers of the world, may be interpreted from one view, as a geographic area, or by a sociological approach, as a process. Geographically this frontier is not merely the narrow line of the Great Wall, a general impression held by Chinese and non-Chinese alike. It is rather a migrating zone of varying depth, a comparatively unsettled area with a low man-to-land ratio, but one which lacks the abundant natural resources and unusual opportunities for individuals to better themselves economically and socially that are found in most other frontiers--Africa, the Americas, and, to a lesser degree, Siberia. The traditional Chinese conception of the frontier is evident in the most commonly used term, pien-chiang, which is closer to the meaning of a "border," a "boundary," or an "edge"--lacking a sense of either depth or process. Historically, in the case of China, the cultural realm and the political state have tended to be more coterminous than in many other expanding or pioneering countries where there is less of a culture break and more of a diffusion or cultural fluidity beyond the border. With China, the state tends to follow cultural penetration and vice-versa. Thus the Mongol frontier in one sense has been an undefined and unstable or transitory boundary between the expanding society of China and the lands of Mongolia, which were broad but also inhospitable to the intensive agricultural methods of the Chinese.

In analyzing the Mongol frontier as a "process," the focus is not upon a narrow line of boundary contact, but upon the social process in which individuals and institutions are changed by the environment, through interaction between different nationalities, and by the events which transpire in the stream of history. Sociologically, China's Mongol frontier was much less a "stage in the development of society" than the American or the Russian frontiers, where new social conditions brought about great changes in old institutions and ideas. For Europeans who settled on the American frontier, a whole new style of life developed. But one sees almost no change in Chinese institutions as they extended into the frontier. Rather, there was a persistence of the old, as district and province (hsien and sheng), and other institutions were set up on the lines of traditional models.

In contrast, as the long-term isolation of Mongolia broke down, which had been imposed in part by geography and in part by Manchu policy, changes took place which were not quite as rapid as those in Meiji Japan, but at the same time not as slow as those of China during the late Ch'ing period. While certain Mongol attitudes and values changed rapidly between the Revolution (1911) and World War II (1945), some institutions were anachronistically perpetuated by such conservatives as Yuan Shih-k'ai, by some Mongol leaders, and by Japanese military administrators. This is not to judge whether the arrested change was good or bad.

In another sense, the China-Mongol frontier has been a "state of mind" and the Great Wall is a fitting psychological symbol for the Chinese side of the frontier as the jumping-off-place into barbarism and outer darkness. To borrow Toynbee's idea of "challenge and response," the frontier of Mongolia has presented such a great threat historically that China's response has been a fixation on the northern "barbarians," a mental set caused by repeated nomadic invasions--such a preoccupation, in fact, that the modern threat from the southeastern sea frontier (<u>hai chiang</u>) and European imperialism was not realized.

The frontier has had a tremendous psychological impact on the indigenous Mongols, as the frontier region became inundated by Chinese colonists. It is the pastoral peoples being forced out or assimilated in the frontier who are subjected to the most traumatic experience. The psychological results are by no means simple and can barely be touched on here. In some cases, Mongol response has been frustration, anger, and a blind, rather disorganized striking out against the new settlers. With closer contact, an earlier ethnocentric superiority complex among the Mongols gave way to feelings of inferiority as Mongols lost control of their environment and as they gained greater insight into the complexities of Chinese administrative institutions and the sophistication of Chinese culture. This attitude arose in many areas where the living standard of the Mongols was depressed as they lost their better pastures. A common phenomenon was a Mongolian aping of Chinese speech, clothing, and general life style. The most notable cases in this regard are in the Tumed areas of western Mongolia (Suiyuan) and the Josoto League of southeastern Mongolia (Jehol). This was accompanied by a tendency, common among minorities worldwide, for some Mongols to resort to opportunism for survival or to gain status and security in the dominant society.

Finally, a definite fatalistic mood arose in the minds of many people when the Chinese Communist takeover led to disillusionment after a brief period of euphoria. A defeatist reaction that standing against the Chinese tide was hopeless was generally justified.

The turn of the century brought a new stage to the China-Mongol frontier when a new Mongolian elite arose among young Mongols educated in Chinese and Japanese schools. They breathed a new enlightenment and a national consciousness, and were quite different in their views from the old hereditary elite. They made very energetic efforts to sponsor reform and even promoted rather revolutionary changes. An example is the case of the

Inner Mongolian Kuomintang organized in 1925, just before the
Northern Expedition (1926). As Mongol nationalism developed,
a sense of urgency arose--an anxiety for the very existence
of the Mongolian culture and people. Complex new combinations
of most of the above Mongol responses to life on the frontier
continued through the period of warlord domination (1916-28)
and the Japanese occupation (1931-45) and into the present
Communist period.

The restriction of Chinese movement into the Mongol frontier was both geographically and politically determined. While the northern frontier has been there for thousands of years, Chinese have not penetrated it in any great numbers until very recently. It has been a shallow frontier, compared to the deep penetration of the American and Russian frontiers. In the span of but two hundred years, the American frontier was penetrated several thousand miles by millions of people. Compared to this deep frontier, China's shallow frontier, limited particularly by the Gobi Desert, has been a negative sort of "challenge of avoidance." It has been quite well known to the Chinese, who have lived with it for centuries, but only a few people have moved into it and then only reluctantly, lacking other acceptable alternatives as population pressure, famine, and political chaos arose. In contrast, the American and Russian frontiers were at first unexplored and relatively unknown, and in the American case, at least, held a "challenge of attraction." Kevin Starr, in his recent book <u>Americans and the California Dream, 1850-1915</u>, projects this idea beautifully when he discusses the dramatic influence of the development of western America. He talks of this frontier as "the cutting edge of the American Dream . . . a symbol of renewal. It was a final frontier: of geography and of expectation." This is a marked contrast to the bleak image of the China-Mongol frontier.

The early modern period of the China frontier was marked by a "Manchu Policy," a conservative, self-serving colonial policy that emphasized the isolation of the frontier beyond the Great Wall and which in many ways protected its inhabitants. There were to be no settlements, no mining, no intermarriage, and no development of Chinese language, education, or trading activity. This was in marked contrast to the conventional colonial frontier policy found in the Americas, Africa, or Russia: economic penetration, exploitation, and fulfillment of the stewardship of the "white man's burden." In time, this Manchu colonial policy of isolation broke down or mutated into a new "Chinese frontier policy," in part because of Chinese commercial interests in Mongolia and in part as a defense against a growing Russian threat in the Amur River region. By 1900 Manchu impotence, population pressures, disruption, strife, and natural disasters in China proper forced millions of people beyond the Wall into Mongol lands. And, while the Chinese frontier served as an indirect safety valve or Malthusian release in alleviating the population pressure in some Chinese provinces under crisis or stress, the potential for settlement beyond the Wall was greatly limited in comparison to the American frontier.

Much of what is unique about American character is attributed to its frontier experience: excessive individualism, blind worship of democratic principles, and arrogant nationalism are listed by some. In contrast, a tentative conclusion is that Chinese frontier experience of migration beyond the Great Wall has made no really significant changes in basic Chinese personality and attitudes or in the social institutions of those involved in the experience.

Thus, apart from the physical environments there was a great contrast in the human element of the Chinese-Mongol as compared to the American frontier experience. The Americans who moved into Indian territory were a product of the European enlightenment; that is, they espoused an open society and ideas of progress and rationality, self-reliance, and individual responsibility for one's actions. Americans had a large degree of autonomy in making such decisions as their marriage arrangement, place of residence, and career. With this orientation, their reaction to frontier experience was quite unique. The Chinese, on the other hand, before the very recent liberating influences of nationalism and Communism, were still products of traditional Chinese folk society. Age took precedence over youth, women were subordinated, the individual had little control over his fate as to marriage, education, and residence. Ideas of progress and change were quite alien, and personal relationships were very particularistic. Life followed a simple traditional formula and the level of superstition and illiteracy was still very high. The conservative Chinese peasant, unlike the American pioneer, conformed much more to a customary model in adapting to frontier life.

In contrast to the colonizing Chinese, anthropological studies will confirm that centuries of development of Mongolian society in the steppe resulted in more freedom for the individual, a higher status for women, and generally a more loosely constructed society. Among the nomads, epic poetry and more emphasis on romantic love also seem to be part of the picture.

The relative isolation of the frontier seems to have conditioned in both Mongols and Americans a certain naivete which was for a time a stumbling block in political or diplomatic relations with others. Both have tended to be less inhibited, more outgoing and straight-forward in personal relationships. Sports and outdoor life appeal to them more than to most people. In sum, the Mongol frontier did not present a combination of physical conditions and cultural traditions that could change basic values or behavior as they were changed in the American West.

In addition to the fact that Chinese experience in penetrating the Mongolian frontier has been limited both in depth of field and extension of time is the point that the pattern of Chinese settlement was generally in sizable groups. Those who moved beyond the Wall soon collected into colonies, established hsien administrative units and recreated the traditional social and political institutions characteristic of China for centuries. Russian and especially American frontier settlement was more scattered and, while a high degree of cooperation occurred, the diffused nature of the migration over great areas was more conducive to an open society with universal values rather than the particularistic type characteristic of traditional China. The most basic determinant in the Chinese case was the traditional institutional conditioning from which the people came. The great stability of the highly integrated Chinese family system was perpetuated in new areas and militated against an open society or an individually determined existence. The projection of the Chinese version of folk society into the frontier meant a comparatively high level of continuity of the unique personality configuration of the Chinese and the Confucian value system, with its associated attitudes and behavior patterns.

Siberian settlement was diffused far across the broad expanse of the railroad line. The shadow of Tzarist control or Stalinist totalitarianism was weakened but never quite removed. Still the Siberian frontier was in a sense the most liberated area in all of Russia, and here were found more creative talent and cultured people than in any frontier of the world. Needless to say, they were not there voluntarily, but nevertheless the Chinese and American frontiers could not compare in this respect.

Lawlessness seems to be a standard feature of frontiers everywhere. The American West was wild and the Mongol frontier early abounded in raiding nomads and more recently in bandits, the so-called "Meng-fei." Both the Chinese and the American frontiers had their share of criminals, but were never populated systematically by colonies of criminals and political prisoners as in Imperial Russia or the Soviet Union.

To Americans the term frontier meant opportunity, an abundance of natural resources, wealth, and upward mobility. Americans were conditioned by their frontier to be shockingly wasteful, and they squandered their natural resources. But Inner Mongolia has been a frontier of frugality. It has meant a difficult life to most of its inhabitants. Life was precarious, always near the subsistence level because of the geographical limitations on agriculture in the steppe and the Gobi. A bad season or a natural disaster frequently brought tragedy. The same was often true of the Indian of the American frontier, but the white man, heir to the science and technology of modern Europe, was the most successful in world history in controlling his frontier environment to bring more comfort, wealth, and longer life. The same technological factors have helped the Russian migrant to at least make the Siberian frontier livable.

The revolutions in science, industry, and commerce have invariably helped the dominant society, while the isolated Mongols in the interior are an example of a people victimized by exclusion from the early stages of modernization. They, like the early inhabitants of the Russian East or the American West, were late in gaining the advantages of science and were thus unable to defend themselves.

The development of railroads into the frontier calls for special mention. The Trans-Siberian Railroad was a spectacular thrust across the largest frontier on earth and continues to contribute to its settlement. The transcontinental railroad of the United States was a great factor in bringing an end to the frontier of North America, except for Canada and Alaska. Railroad building in Inner Mongolia after the turn of the century was a primary cause in bringing new Chinese settlement and pressure on the Mongols and in precipitating a whole new stage in Mongol-Chinese frontier history.

One might conclude from the comments made that each frontier is a unique experience and that while there are similarities in the various cases the differences are often more significant. Needless to say, by a comparative study of various world frontiers we will gain greater insight into our own experience in western America.

PART II:
THE CASES OF WANG T'UNG-CH'UN, PRIVATE LAND
DEVELOPER, AND I KU, GOVERNMENT COLONIZATION PROMOTOR

Wang T'ung-ch'un: Pioneer Land
Developer in Inner Mongolia

Frontier men whose names are remembered are often self-made men. Some have shady backgrounds, many have great motivation, and the most capable have great ability as developers or entrepreneurs. As a specific case study on the China-Mongol frontier, the career of Wang T'ung-ch'un (1851-1925) is particularly interesting. For data we are indebted to the outstanding scholar, Ku Che-kang, who became interested in the important Mongolian separatist movement in the early 1930s and gathered materials and made interviews to learn more of the complex history of the North China border area.

Wang T'ung-ch'un's career represents an early stage of private frontier land development from 1875 to 1900. When he came to western Mongolia there were very few Chinese settlers, but when he died in 1925, just three years before Suiyuan became a province, millions lived there. The Mongols had been pushed back, Outer Mongolia had separated itself from China, and the stage was set for a nationalistic Inner Mongolian autonomous movement.

Wang T'ung-ch'un came of humble origins in Hopei Province. Typical of the frontier, he had no formal education and was illiterate throughout his life. As a youth of sixteen, Wang fled to the frontier to escape arrest for killing a fellow villager and settled in the Ho-t'ao area. This was a fertile region north of the Great Wall and fairly deep in Mongol territory. In the early Ch'ing Dynasty it was still quite unsettled by Chinese farmers. Wang was an early pioneer in the area, but a number of others preceded him and soon came to oppose him when they felt threatened by his dynamic activity.

Earlier in the mid-eighteenth century, a group of fishermen from the Yellow River, becoming aware of the fertility of the Ho-t'ao land, began to plant and irrigate it with great success. In 1833 the Yellow River flooded and changed its course to the south, creating a large new section of fertile land with a new layer of top soil and good potential for irrigated farming. Peasants from the neighboring province of Shansi, learning of the new development, began to migrate into the area to bring it under cultivation. Their efforts were successful, but development was rather limited until Kao Yu-yuan, a Ssuchuanese, settled in the Ho-t'ao with his wife from frontier Kansu. Coming from an area famous for its irrigation system, it was only natural that Kao build the first modern canal in the Mongol frontier area of Ulanchab (Suiyuan). This canal (ho), named Lao Kao in tribute to its pioneer founder, so increased productivity as to eventually support a sizable Chinese population in the South Urad Banner area, later to be organized as An-pei District, a borderland community.

In 1874 Wang T'ung-ch'un began to work for Kao Yu-yuan, and later married his daughter. He soon began to lease Mongol land on his own and settled in southern Ulanchab at Lung-hsing-ch'ang. Here, in what was to later become the important center of Wu-yuan District, he developed the headquarters or base for what was to become a virtual empire--and for Wang a very impressive career as a frontier land developer. In 1881 Wang built his first canal. Five years later he built another over thirty-five miles in length and established himself as an independent developer. Hundreds of refugees and poor peasants were recruited to come in to the land to bring it under cultivation.

During the last quarter of the nineteenth century, the main era of private land developers on the western sector of the Mongol border, Wang T'ung-ch'un was by no means the only man developing frontier land, but he was the most important. There were perhaps a half dozen other fairly important men developing canals and bringing settlers into Ulanchab and the northern Ordos regions. The competition was keen, and reminiscent of the American West was the struggle over irrigation water and the resort to rifles and pistols with the resulting bloodshed and death. Wang became the most powerful figure in the region by gathering army deserters, fugitives, and gunmen and equipping them with modern weapons to form a private army. Frontier feuding and warfare was eventually somewhat reduced when Wang became dominant in the area, powerful enough to control five of the eight regions of the entire Ho-t'ao area. Eventually this gave him, according to one report, control of over 250,000 acres, including 70 farm villages. His activity changed the entire environment of this part of Inner Mongolia and, as his work spread, it had an important economic and political impact further south in the Dalat Banner of Yeke-juu League, south of the Yellow River loop.

Wang's approach to canal building and land development will not be detailed here, but it should be noted that the testimony available establishes him as a most capable hydraulic engineer with a keen talent for determining elevations and for making careful judgments as to how to use water and which land could be most successfully cultivated.

As for the character of Wang T'ung-ch'un, he was an authoritarian, paternalistic man who seems to have provoked either great admiration or great hatred from those with whom he had contact. On one hand, he ate and worked with his men and was very generous in assisting peasants in relief work. He helped tens of thousands during the great famine of 1891 in north China and again in 1901. Many refugees and migrants came into his area, particularly from Hopei, Shantung, and Shansi provinces. However, it seems that Wang's assistance was not out of pure charity, for at one point the government sought his arrest on suspicion of using migrants to build a warlord army and a private kingdom. Estimates of the number of men he could recruit as a personal army range from twenty to fifty thousand at the peak of his career. His discipline was strict and his workers were severely regimented. It is reported that even his daughter, with bound feet, supervised labor gangs with a rifle, and that he exercised the power of life or death over his men. He was merciless to his enemies and those who opposed him. According to reports gathered by Professor Ku, over three thousand people were executed by him in a single year.

Another criticism of Wang T'ung-ch'un by his contemporaries was of his brutal exploitation of the Mongols. There seems to have been no problem at first in his successful negotiation of land leases with Mongol leaders, but later, as he became something of a local warlord with a personal army, he moved from diplomacy to the use of force to exact leases in perpetuity--for as long as ten thousand years, it is claimed. In other cases, he simply forced the Mongols from their land, causing them either to move farther north beyond the Yin-shan Mountains in Ulanchab territory, or farther south into the desert-like regions of the Ordos Banners. In either case, they were deprived of their best grazing lands. As good pastures were cultivated and as the Mongols were impoverished, bloody incidents occurred and tension between the Chinese and Mongols grew.

Most Chinese writers rationalize Wang's actions, explaining that the Mongols were not developing their land and, therefore, it was proper for the Chinese to develop it for them. In assessing the activity of Wang T'ung-ch'un over several decades, one cannot help but admire his broad accomplishments, while at the same time condemning the way in which he exploited both Chinese settlers and Mongol herders. Ku Che-kang's judgment confirms that the Mongols did indeed suffer from Wang's development, but not as much as they did later when government officials became involved in frontier land development, with a rise in corruption and exploitation.

Wang T'ung-ch'un's relationship with the Mongols could not have been one of total alienation, for some of his early land leases from the Mongol banners seem to have come voluntarily and are explained in part by the fact that the nomadic princes were in great need financially. They were hard pressed for income to make annual trips to Peking and to pay tribute to the Manchu court. They did not foresee the long-range threat of Chinese settlement to their pastoral life. Chinese land development was like the camel that at first merely got its nose into the tent, but later moved in entirely.

Conflict was not limited to that between Chinese and Mongols, for the Mongols themselves had disputes over such problems as the jurisdiction of pastures, and Wang was called upon to help arbitrate Mongol problems, possibly more out of deference to his power than in a hope for justice.

An interesting example of the recognition of Wang's work by the Mongols came at the peak of his career around 1890. In 1891 the Jebtsundamba, great Living Buddha of Urga, requested him to come to Outer Mongolia to build canals. Wang accepted the request and went to Outer Mongolia with some thousand workers, but the details of this undertaking are not available and the reasons for its failure are not clear.

Apart from his conflict with other private land developers in western Mongolia, Wang also came in conflict with the Catholic missionaries who by coincidence began their own work in western Mongolia in 1875, just one year after Wang himself came on the scene as a young man. The Belgian fathers (C.I.C.M.) gained influence by establishing commune-like agricultural colonies and by promoting education, medical work, and famine relief. As their influence and landholdings grew, particularly after the Boxer Rebellion in 1900, they eventually came into conflict with Wang. The details of this relationship are lacking, but one incident in the far southern part of the Ordos, in the Ujin Banner, may serve as an example. As part of the indemnity for damages incurred in the Boxer Rebellion, the Catholics were given Mongol salt reserves or production areas. The missionaries decided to sell the salt works but refused to sell it to Wang T'ung-ch'un because of previous conflicts between him and the Church.

The Boxer Rebellion brought significant changes to land development in western Mongolia. On the one hand, the Catholic missionaries gained control over important tracts of land, and Mongols still note this as a cause of antipathy to the Church during later years, mainly because it increased the flow of agricultural settlers. But even more important was the appearance on the scene of large-scale government-directed land development and peasant settlement, replacing the earlier domination of the field by private land developers.

Following the turn of the century, Ch'ing government policy began to promote Chinese colonization in the border regions. The greatest number of Chinese peasants flowed into the Mongol lands of eastern Mongolia, particularly Josoto and Juu-uda Leagues (Jehol) and farther north. In western Mongolia, the area of our focus here, the governor-general of Shansi Province, Ch'en Ch'un-hsuan, proposed that the government develop Mongol lands. He set up an office himself for this purpose in Suiyuan. It was natural that such a proposal come from this quarter, in view of the fact that Inner Mongolia, through much of the modern period, had been virtually an economic colony of Shansi Province, particularly after the rise of the warlord Yen Hsi-shan.

The key figure in this new stage of government-directed frontier development was I-ku, a Manchu official who was appointed land commissioner for Inner Mongolia and governor-general (Chiang-chun) of Kweihua, which became Suiyan Province in 1928 with the establishment of the Nanking government. He was concurrently a grand-secretary (shang-shu) of the Li-fan yuan and had close connections with Jung Lu, a court favorite of the dowager empress. This lasted until 1907 when I-ku's career was suddenly cut short by the greatest frontier development scandal of the late Ch'ing period.

I-ku arrived on the Mongol frontier in 1903 and found that Governor Ch'en of Shansi had the year before established a Land Development Bureau (Feng-ning ya-huang chu). This office I-ku immediately took over, reorganizing and coordinating it with the East-West Land Development Corporation (Tung-Hsi-lu k'en-wu kung-ssu), a private company that he established specifically to make money in land reclamation on the frontier. A real conflict of interest was the fact that I-ku was both head of the government land office established to survey and register Mongol lands, and also the head of a private company organized to reap profits of land development by taking large tracts from the Mongols and selling them to Chinese settlers.

I-ku immediately saw that Wang T'ung-ch'un was a very important figure in the region and a possible threat to his plans--a man who must be removed in order that I-ku himself might take over the dominant role as land developer. However, I-ku did not make a direct attack on Wang, whose position was too formidable. Rather, as a diversion, he enlisted Wang's services with an assignment as chief engineer of the Land Development Bureau for the purpose of using his experience in canal building.

But Wang was not deceived. He immediately recognized I-ku's objectives and those of the crowd of officials who had followed him to the frontier. Wang's counter-strategy was to ostensibly cooperate with the government men while actually taking every precaution to prevent them from confiscating his property or undermining his position. Wang's strategy is seen in the case of a government-sponsored Ch'ang-che canal project. Wang's work crews dug the canal in such a way that it was not only useless for irrigating the land around it, but also allowed water to flow into other canals, flooding them and making them useless.

A crisis finally arose when Wang T'ung-ch'un came into conflict with I-ku's man Yao Hsueh-ching, magistrate of a new administrative jurisdiction established in the Ho-t'ao with its seat in Wu-yuan. Yao Hsueh-ching was at the time the general director of land reclamation for the western leagues (Hsi-meng k'en-wu tsung-pan). The problem came when Wang refused to allow government use of his private canals, which provoked Yao to dispatch a contingent of troops to Wang's home to force his compliance. By such means the government took over the irrigation system, without which the land would be useless. Then immediately an irrigation bureau was created, which began to tax the farmers for the use of the water. As the taxes became burdensome, some farmers gave up their land, which lapsed into deserted fields.

Wang's troubles were only beginning. Some of his old enemies came back to haunt him, one of the first being Ch'in-ssu, a Mongol prince of the Dalad Banner whom Wang had earlier exploited. In his concern, Wang hired a professional killer to eliminate the Mongol prince in February of 1903. I-ku's men seized this opportunity. Pretending to be Wang's friends and counselors, they expressed a willingness to help him clear himself from charges of killing the Mongol prince and of extorting Mongol lands. The officials contrived to have Wang sign a paper. Being illiterate, he did not realize that he was signing over a large part of his property to the Land Bureau.

Wang was finally convicted of various charges and served five years in jail. He narrowly escaped death as all prisoners were ordered executed when the 1911 revolution broke out. Of the prisoners, Wang alone escaped, so Professor Ku reported, and returned to his old home on the Mongol frontier, where he trained local militia for a new governor-general at Kweihua under the Republic. In the fall of 1913 Wang and his troops helped to repel Outer Mongolian forces that attacked Ulanchab League in an attempt to bring that area over to the side of Outer Mongolia in its new movement for independence.

Governor-General I-ku and Government Land Development in Western Mongolia

As a case study in the western Mongol frontier history the land-development scandal of I-ku is very complex, and only a few high points can be touched upon here. Fortunately, detailed materials are available on this case in the form of an official investigation report by Grand-Secretary (shang-shu) Lu Wen-jui, who was sent to investigate I-ku's activities. The investigation led to I-ku's conviction, dismissal from office, and imprisonment. As mentioned above, I-ku, who was appointed governor-general over the Ulanchab and Yekejuu (Ordos) areas and concurrently land commissioner for development in Inner Mongolia, was a Manchu official with support right in the Ch'ing Court. I-ku's main assignment was to make a survey of Mongol lands and to register them in order to open them for sale and settlement. Though the Land Development Agency was set up in August 1902, it was not until June 1903 that it really began its work.

Initially, the concentration was on opening the lands of the Hangin and Dalad Banners of the Yeke-juu League (Ordos), with particular attention to building irrigation canals. In 1905, as the work progressed and settlers came in, the general headquarters were moved from Kweihua city to Paot'ou, just a short distance north across the river from the Dalad Banner, where much of the settlement work was taking place. Branch bureaus were set up in four or five places in the Ordos and in several places in the Ulanchab League.

The original plan called for development first in the three Urad banners of Ulanchab, but here the six Mongol banners united together and resisted the move to colonize their lands. It took considerable persuasion and pressure from special representatives of the government to each of the Ulanchab banners to constrain them to cooperate. In 1906 this league finally agreed to land registration and within a year it was completed. In contrast, according to the report, some of the banners in Yekejuu League dispatched representatives to contact government officials at Kweihua and voluntarily requested a land registration and the opening of areas for settlement. These were banners in the western part of the Ordos, and their action, if the report is accurate, may be accounted for by the fact that they had experienced less pressure from Chinese colonization and were not representative of all of the Ordos banners. In the Jungar Banner to the east, for example, a leader named Monghejiya (Mon-k'en-chi'ya) led a group in an attack to destroy the government land office in that banner, and land development had to be put under the jurisdiction of a special government representative. Later land development in the Ushin and Jasag banners was handled in the same way.

The government land office over which Governor I-ku presided was active for only five years before its closure in April 1908. During this period I-ku supervised the investment in land development of near 550,000 liang of silver, almost entirely government funds, mostly for the building of canals. There was great activity in land sales and peasant settlement, but the government not only did not realize a return on its investment, but actually lost money because of the misuse of funds by I-ku. I-ku's private land company manipulated the price of land, both in purchases from the government agency and in sales to peasant settlers, in order to monopolize benefits for I-ku and his men in the process. I-ku forceably took over private canal systems and fraudulently dispossessed private land developers who had moved into the area before there was a government office for land registration. In shrewd canal development projects, I-ku gained double funding for the same work, squeezing money from farmers on the one hand and petitioning the government for funds on the other. In some cases I-ku's private company by-passed the government land office and monopolized choice Mongol lands for itself. In other cases the company paid the government agency for a piece of land which actually was far larger than represented in the purchase contract. In a key area, I-ku appointed a man who was managing director for his private development corporation as concurrent head of the local branch office of the government land bureau--a clear conflict of interest. It should be noted that I-ku's initial financing for his private land company came from profits made in colonization of pasture lands farther east in the Chakhar League, where I-ku had organized a separate land company and made a fortune in the sale and settlement of Mongol lands.

In addition to manipulating finances and land deeds, I-ku dealt harshly with Mongolian leaders. In the Hangin Banner, for example, the Jasagh, or ruling Mongol prince, was removed from his office at I-ku's instigation for resisting the colonization of his land. Then, when the land in question in this banner was purchased, I-ku used government revenue which he controlled to pay the land agency for the property, rather than using the funds of his private company. In other Mongol areas, Dalad Banner for one, land was not purchased outright, but was acquired on a perpetual lease arrangement. In some such areas there were large private land operators--pioneers who had preceded the government and were acting as middlemen-- leasing land from the Mongols and renting it out to Chinese farmers. In at least one important instance involving large tracts of valuable land, those of Wang T'ung-ch'un, I-ku forced the transfer of the private leases to his company, using, as a lever, blackmail and his control of the canal system, without which the land was useless.

In the whole process, it was the Mongols who lost most. Their lands were taken over, supposedly by purchase or lease, although actually the Mongols did not even receive the money due them. In one instance, I-ku's land company retained 15,000 _liang_ of silver as a sort of forced investment in the land company's operation. Another 20,000 _liang_ of Mongolian money was paid to the regional military training bureau as a "contribution" by the Mongols. Again, in the same case, I-ku's office withheld another 17,000 _liang_ from the Mongols, which he said he would give to the local Chinese merchants for Yeke-juu Banner debts, debts which were already contested by the Mongols.

Governor-General I-ku and Chinese officials are by no means the only ones open to criticism. In many cases, Mongol officials sold public land belonging to the banner and in other ways reaped personal benefits. There is the Mongol official Mergenbu (Mei-le-k'en-pu) of the Hangin Banner, whom I-ku bought off to assist him in gaining concessions in that banner's lands. Another case is the Buddhist lama Wangdonnima (Wang-te-ni-ma), who was promoted and bribed to assist in opening his banner lands of Ushin. However, the Mongols of this banner were so infuriated by his actions that their resistance eventually forced a cancelation of the deal. One of the worst incidents occurred in the Jungar Banner where one

Dampil (Tan-p'i-erh) organized resistance to the land development program and led a revolt. Troops were sent to crush the rebellion and to arrest Dampil. His execution by Governor I-ku was one important factor which precipitated the government's general investigation of I-ku's operations, which led eventually to his dismissal and imprisonment.

More important than the fate of the few individuals mentioned, and the many others who could be cited, was the fact that the relations between the Chinese and the Mongols in the border area greatly deteriorated. Several years after I-ku's removal (1908), most banner areas of western Mongolia supported the Outer Mongolian movement for independence (1911). Tens of thousands of Chinese also were greatly distressed because the irrigation canal system taken over by the government from private operators during I-ku's period declined without maintenance, and eventually much of it became useless. Thus in the long run the general decline in farmland and pastures of the area hurt both the Chinese and the Mongols. This general development is an important predisposing factor in the movement of the Mongols in the 1920s and 1930s to try to gain greater control over their own fate. Important results were the rise of Mongolian nationalism, the organization of the Inner Mongolian Kuomintang with support from both Sun Yat-sen and the Comintern, and Prince Demchugdungrub's (De Wang) movement for autonomy, all of which are beyond the scope of this discussion.

REFERENCES

Ku Che-kang, "Wang T'ung-ch'un kai-fa Ho-t'ao chi" (An account of Wang T'ung-ch'un's development of the Ho-t'ao area), Yu-kung pan-yueh-kan (Yu-kung Biweekly), 2, no. 12 (24 April 1935).

Meng Shih-ming, "Ho-t'ao nung-tien chui-ti kai-fa yen-ke" (The general history in the development of the land and irrigation canals in Ho-t'ao), Yu-kung pan-yueh-kan, 10, nos. 49, 50 (1 November 1936).

Wang Chi, "Ho-t'ao ch'u-tao chih k'ai-chun yen-ke" (The general history of the construction of the irrigation canals in Ho-t'ao area), Yu-kung pan-yueh-kan, 7, nos. 8, 9 (1 July 1937).

Wang Chi, "Wang T'ung-ch'un hsien-sheng yueh-shih" (Unrecorded stories about Wang T'ung-ch'un), Yu-kung pan-yueh-kan, 4, no. 7 (1 July 1937).

Wu Pao-san, "Wang Lo-yu hsien-sheng te t'an-hua" (A talk with Mr. Wang Lo-yu), Yu-kung pan-yueh-kan, 4, no. 7 (24 April 1934).

The Paradox of Mormon Folklore
William A. Wilson

Each culture needs means of expressing its innermost dreams, aspirations, and fears, and methods of social control. In many cultures--Mormon included--folklore is one means of serving those functions. In this essay, William A. "Bert" Wilson, associate professor of English at Brigham Young University, has explained a number of ways in which folklore fills those roles in Mormon culture.

Professor Wilson's principal point is that though the historical factuality of folklore stories is irrelevant, its psychological accuracy is crucial to understanding the culture. Through folklore, the student of Mormon culture can discover important attitudes and concerns. Beyond this, folklore provides a means of acting out unfulfilled fantasies and deflating pomposity.

Folklore, as Professor Wilson has argued, provides two necessary cultural values. It serves as a means of social regulation and is a source of psychological release. Both of these are undoubtedly necessary in any culture. Thus stories of the dire consequences of sacrilegious acts and attitudes, those which emphasize the need for faithful diligence, and those which deflate pomposity are necessary to the successful functioning of Mormon culture.

As I began work on this paper, I asked a number of friends what they would like to know about Mormon folklore. The responses I got were at such cross purposes the task ahead seemed hopeless. Finally, Richard Anderson solved my problem by confessing that he knew next to nothing about the subject. "I would like to know," he said, "what Mormon folklore is and what you fellows do with it." In this paper I should like to answer Richard's questions. I shall tell you what I, at least, consider Mormon folklore to be; I shall try to demonstrate what those of us who study it do with it; and I shall try to persuade you that what we do is worth doing, providing significant insight into our culture that we cannot always get in other ways.

In the 130 years since the word "folklore" was coined,[1] folklorists have been trying unsuccessfully to decide what the word means. I shall not solve the problem here. Yet if we are to do business with each other, we must come to some common understanding of terms. Briefly, I consider folklore to be the unofficial part of Mormon culture. When a Sunday School teacher reads to his class from an approved lesson manual, he is giving them what the Correlation Committee at least would call official religion; but when he illustrates the lesson with an account of the Three Nephites which he learned from his mother, he is giving them unofficial religion. Folklore, then, is that part of our culture that is passed through time and space by the process of oral transmission (by hearing and repeating) rather than by institutionalized means of learning or by the mass media.

Of course, not everything that we transmit orally is folklore. We distinguish folklore from other forms of verbal communication by clearly discernible structure. We are all familiar with the "Once upon a time" that signals the beginning of a fairy tale and the "And they lived happily ever after" that marks its end. The markers that set off other forms of folklore are often more subtle, but they are nevertheless there, and when we hear the initial signal, most of us know immediately that conversation is going to be interrupted by the telling of a tale. Further, not only is folklore in general set off from regular conversation by its structure, but also the different forms of folklore (for example, ballad, folktale, legend) are separated from each other by the distinctive ordering of their parts. Thus a Nephite story, reduced to its basic elements, is quite a different creature, structurally, from a story about J. Golden Kimball. It is because of this structural patterning, among other things, that we are justified in considering folklore to be literature. Another reason, as we shall see, is that through these narrative patterns we come to terms with some of our most significant Mormon experience.

To suggest that folklore is literature is to suggest that it is fiction; to suggest that it is fiction is to suggest also that it is not true, that it does not recount history accurately. This suggestion will not trouble many when we apply it to folksongs or to humorous anecdotes, which we really don't consider factual; but when we apply it to stories of the Three Nephites or to accounts of visits to or from the spirit world or to divine help in genealogical research, then eyebrows arch all over the place. And this brings me once again to Richard Anderson, who asked: "If we have three oral accounts of something Joseph Smith did, does that mean it's folklore?"

The answer to that question depends on the antecedent of the pronoun *it*. If the pronoun refers to the actual event that started the stories, the answer is clearly no. The event is whatever the event was, and the folklorist will leave to the historian the task of deciphering it. But if the pronoun refers not to the event but to the orally circulating account of it, the answer is yes. The account is, or is on the way to becoming, folklore.

Folklore comes into being through a process we call communal re-creation. In general the materials of Mormon folklore come from three places: they are borrowed from others and then adapted to fit the contours of our culture; they sometimes originate, as Joseph Fielding Smith said, speaking of Nephite stories, from the vivid imaginations of some of our people;[2] and they develop from actual happenings. But whatever the source, the stories become folklore when they are taken over by the people and are reshaped as they are passed from person to person.

This communal re-creation occurs in two ways. First, the stories are reshaped to fit the structural patterns available to the narrators. My mother, a devout Mormon not easily given to criticism, complained the other day that all the talks of returned missionaries sounded the same. What she had perceived was that the return-home address is a traditional form into which the missionary must fit his personal experiences, distorting them, or at least carefully selecting them, to fit the pattern. The process is similar to that which one follows when he attempts to develop his personal experience into a short story. To be successful, he must distort the experience to make it fit the structural requirements of the form.

Consider, for example, the stories of the Three Nephites. The basic structure of these stories seems to be this: someone has a problem; a stranger appears; the stranger solves the problem; the stranger miraculously disappears. A story may have more to it than this, but it must have these features. Any account that is taken into the Nephite cycle will be adjusted (probably unconsciously) to fit the pattern. The remarkable disappearance is particularly interesting. I see no compelling reasons why the Nephites must disappear. In Book of Mormon times they were thrown into prison, into dens of wild beasts, and into furnaces, and in none of these instances did they solve their problems by disappearing. But in the modern stories, they vanish from the back seats of speeding cars; they vaporize before one's eyes; or they walk away and someone later tracing their footsteps in the snow finds that they abruptly end. The Nephites disappear, I believe, because the story requires it. The disappearance is the climax toward which the narrative builds, overshadowing in many instances the kindly deeds the Nephites came to perform in the first place.

The second way in which communal re-creation occurs is that the stories are reshaped (again probably unconsciously) to reflect the attitudes, values, and concerns of the people telling the stories. In 1962 a student in John Sorenson's BYU anthropology class collected the following item from one of her teachers:

> Brother James Rencher was a very devout man, who, in all of his spare time, read and reread the Book of Mormon. However, no matter how many times he pored over the book, there remained ten questions concerning it which he could not answer. Every year during the fall, the Renchers moved down into town to escape the harsh winter. One day in October, 1898, Brother Rencher was moving some furniture and provisions down the mountain, when it began to snow. All of a sudden, a strange man appeared several yards in front of him, and asked for a ride. The stranger climbed into the wagon, and immediately began talking about the Book of Mormon. During the next few minutes he answered all of Brother Rencher's questions about the book. Then he jumped out of the wagon and started to walk away. Being concerned that the stranger would freeze in the cold snow, Brother Rencher went after him. He traced the man's footprints to the top of the mountain; there they suddenly disappeared.[3]

I have several accounts of this story quite similar to this one, except that in some not even the general authorities could answer Rencher's questions and in some Rencher was from Pine Valley while in others he was from Heber City or from Idaho. In two versions of the story published by Austin Fife in 1940, Rencher picked up an old hitchhiker who explained political and religious matters "to his satisfaction just perfectly."[4] These accounts suggest that the story once had a double theme—politics and religion. A version of the story collected just last year emphasizes the politics:

> Brother Rencher was closing up a campground
> and left to go home. After he had been
> driving in the mountains for a way, he came
> across a man who seemed to appear from no
> where. They were out in an area where there
> was no one living and very few people passed
> that way. Brother Rencher in order to start
> conversation asked the man what he thought
> of the political parties. The man, who turned
> out to be one of the three Nephites, answered:
> "They are both as corrupt as hell."

What we see here then is that different people, or groups of people, perceive the important "message" of an item differently, and as they continue to tell the story they drop or add details to strengthen what they consider to be important in the story.[5]

Another example of the shifting shape of folklore lies closer to home. Most of us will remember the turbulent period in late 1969 and early 1970 when BYU athletic teams and the marching Cougarettes met violent demonstrations in neighboring schools, when a spate of stories was circulating about bus loads of Black Panthers making their way to the state to blow up Mountain Dell Reservoir and to invade Temple Square, and when some people feared to travel beyond the state's boundaries because they had heard gory stories of people with Utah license plates being stopped by Blacks and beaten up. Emotions were intensified by the revival and rapid circulation of John Taylor's apocryphal Horse Shoe Prophecy. (This prophecy was first written down in 1951 by Edward Lunt, who said that in 1903 or 1904 he had learned it from his mother, who said that she had received it from President Taylor in 1885.)[6] In Lunt's account, President Taylor supposedly saw a day of great trouble and warfare striking the saints, with "blood running down the gutters of Salt Lake City as though it were water." As versions of the prophecy began to multiply during the violence of 1969 and 1970, a new motif was added to it--the notion that the blood would run in the gutters because of racial warfare. For example, an employee of Seminaries and Institutes stated

> that it was common knowledge among teachers
> in the Church educational system that a
> confrontation with Black Panthers was going
> to take place in the streets of Salt Lake
> City and that this would be a fulfillment
> of the prophecy that Blacks would wreak
> havoc in the streets of Zion. He said that
> this prophecy was given to President Taylor.

> It was common knowledge from reliable
> sources [he said] that Blacks and hippies
> were arming themselves in the canyons
> east of the city and that the FBI had un-
> covered plans by revolutionaries to hit
> Salt Lake City with a violence campaign.

Another individual, a stockbroker who claimed he did not believe the part about Negroes, stated:

> John Taylor is supposed to have said that
> the Negroes will march to the west and that
> they will tear down the gates to the temple,
> ravage the women therein, and destroy and
> desecrate the temple. Then the Mormon boys
> will pick up their deer rifles and destroy
> the Negroes, and that's when the blood will
> run down the street.

On March 30, 1970, the First Presidency, concerned by the growing emotionalism, released a statement in which they denounced the Horse Shoe Prophecy and urged members to school their feelings.⁷ In their statement, the First Presidency quoted a memorandum from the Church Historian's office which pointed out that of the five copies of the prophecy on file in that office no two were identical in wording and that the statement about Negroes was in one of the copies but not in the others, "particularly" not in the version signed by Lunt. What the First Presidency actually did was conduct a small-scale folklore study. They discovered, as we have discovered with the James Rencher stories, that as stories are passed from person to person they are "adjusted" to reflect the concerns and to fit the predispositions of the people.

What I am saying, then, is that while folklore may be factually false, it is psychologically true. Students of Mormon culture turn to it not to discover the ledger-book truths of history but to fathom the truths of the human heart and mind. The truths that we find may not always please us, but if we really want to understand ourselves I know of no better place to turn than to folklore.

I say this with some hesitation because I am well aware that Mormon literature, belles lettres, gives us good insight into the Mormon ethos. But I am convinced that Mormon folklore gives us a still clearer view. My reason for believing this is simple: the works of Mormon belles lettres are the creative products of individuals; the works of Mormon folk literature are the creative products of the people, constantly being reshaped, as we have seen above, to mirror contemporary values, anxieties, and social practices. The Mormon poet or short-story writer, however much he draws on his Mormon background and however much he discusses his works in process with his Mormon friends, still gives us his own <u>individual</u> interpretation of our culture, an interpretation, I might add, that is elitist in approach. On the other hand, an item of Mormon folklore, to have become folklore, must have moved from the individual expression of its originator to the communal expression of those who preserve it, losing, through the process of communal re-creation described above, the marks of individual invention and assuming in time a form that reflects the consensus of the group.

In a recent BYU address, N. Scott Momaday made this point far more eloquently than I when, speaking of a Kiowa Indian tale, he said: "As many times as that story has been told it was always but one generation removed from extinction."[8] As soon as any story, Kiowa or not, ceases to appeal to its hearers then, it dies, or it is changed to reflect a new reality. No two tellers, of course, will ever relate the same story the same way; but if that story is to live, they cannot, in the telling of it, depart too far from the value center of the audience whose approval they seek.

I have been dealing so far with the revelatory nature of Mormon folklore and have ignored its functional role. That is, I have been discussing what folk stories mean to the student of Mormon culture, but I have said nothing about what they mean to the people who tell them and listen to them, nothing about the force of folklore in the lives of human beings. In the remainder of my time, I should like to discuss the influence of Mormon folklore on Church members, as it functions to reinforce Church dogma and practice, to sanction approved forms of behavior, and to give people a sense of stability in an unstable world.

In 1694 Puritan divines Increase and Cotton Mather and the Fellows of Harvard College instructed the New England clergy to record the remarkable providences that would show the hand of God in their lives. "The things to be esteemed <u>memorable</u>," they said, "are especially <u>all unusual accidents</u>, in the heaven, or earth, or water: all wonderful <u>deliverances</u> of the distressed: <u>mercies</u> to the godly; <u>judgments</u> on the wicked; and more glorious fulfillment of either the <u>promises</u> or the <u>threatenings</u> in the Scriptures of truth; with <u>apparitions</u>, <u>possessions</u>, inchantments, and all extraordinary things wherein the existence and agency of the <u>invisible world</u> is more sensibly demonstrated."[9] A friend of mine said this passage reminded him of instructions on how to keep a Book of Remembrance. And indeed we Mormons, like the Puritans, seem eager to seek evidence of the invisible world, not simply because we like sensational stories but because, as Cracroft and Lambert point out, "the Mormon world is a God-made, man-centered world" and because "each Latter-day Saint in his personal life is challenged to bring forth evidence that supports this belief."[10] But in the stories we tell, we are seeking not just evidence that God lives but also that his programs are inspired and that he expects us to follow them. Stories about genealogical research and temple work illustrate this point well.

We are all familiar with the plethora of stories genealogy workers tell to encourage others to keep up the pursuit of their dead ancestors. For example, two LDS men driving to a conference pick up a man (later thought to be a Nephite) who urges them to do their genealogy work and then disappears from the back seat of the car. On another occasion, a lady who has trouble tracing her genealogical line prays for help. While she is out of the room where her typewriter is located, she hears its keys clicking. Investigating, she finds the missing information typed in the proper places on her pedigree chart. And so the stories go: A stranger appears to a man in the temple and warns him to get busy on his genealogy because the time is short. A Nephite brings to the temple genealogical sheets that a couple had left home on the table. A man is instructed by a stranger to visit a graveyard, where he finds his missing family names. A man is instructed to go to a pawn shop, where he finds his genealogical data in a Bible. In exchange for a meal, a Nephite gives a lady a book containing information which she needs to extend her family genealogy. And a woman finds the missing names she has been searching for in a newspaper left mysteriously in her car. All of these stories make two main points: first, genealogical research must be important because the Lord helps people complete it; and, second, if one keeps struggling faithfully ahead, not getting discouraged, he will eventually succeed.

If genealogical research is important, so, of course is temple work, both for oneself and for one's ancestors. And once again circulating oral narratives stress the importance of this work. For example, couples who have not been sealed in the temple are visited by mysterious strangers (usually Nephites), who warn them to make haste in getting their work done. Couples who have been to the temple pick up old men along the highways who urge them to attend the temple often because time is short, warn them that otherwise they will not be ready when the Savior comes, and then disappear. Stories are legion about temple workers missing one of the names on a list and then having this mistake made known in a miraculous way. But the most widely circulated story today is probably the following:

A lady in Salt Lake City, Utah, was desirous of going to the temple but was afraid to leave her children at home alone. She hadn't been able to locate a suitable baby-sitter but finally she did. She went to the temple a little apprehensive and about halfway through the session she felt so uneasy that she got up to leave. As she got to the back of the room, a temple worker stopped her to find out what the matter was. She, the lady, said she felt like she was urgently needed at home. The temple worker promised her that if she would return to her seat and finish the session everything would be fine. So she did. After the session was over she hurried home, and sure enough, there were fire engines and police cars all around her house. As she was running to her house, a neighbor lady stopped her and explained that her daughter had fallen into the ditch and couldn't be found. As the lady came to the house, there was her daughter soaking wet and crying. Her mother grabbed her and hugged her. After, the little girl gave her mother a note and explained that the lady who'd pulled her out of the ditch had given it to her. There on the note was the name of the lady for whom this woman had gone through the temple that day.

In some versions of this story it is the new baby-sitter herself who pulls the child from the water. In these instances the sitter then disappears and the mother later recalls that the person whose work she had done in the temple that day had the same name as the baby-sitter.[11] In one version the mother and her husband, though faithful in other duties, have not been attending the temple and finally decide to go only after their bishop makes a personal request. In another version the couple actually call home, learn that their child is missing, but, after praying and getting a feeling that all will be well, remain and complete the session. But whatever form the story takes, it serves always, as one informant said, "as a testimony to the truthfulness of temple work."

These stories, then, not only mirror our concern with genealogical research and temple work, they also reinforce our belief that these pursuits are of God and thus persuade us more eagerly to participate in them.

In one of the most common stories of the Three Nephites, one of the old men visits a home, asks for nourishment, is given it, and then blesses the home with health and prosperity. But in one instance the lady of the house hasn't "time to bother" with her visitor; as a result she loses some of her children to the flu. In another, a lady who turns a beggar away has her lawn overrun with Bermuda grass. Stories like these are what Cotton Mather called "judgments on the wicked." They teach us to do right by showing us what happens to us when we don't. Many of them have to do with blasphemy and graphically demonstrate, in the words of one informant, that "the Lord will not be mocked." For example, in 1962 two priests from California decided to baptize a goat; they were struck dumb and haven't talked yet. In Idaho, the wayward son of a stake president consecrated a glass of beer; he passed out immediately, fell into a coma, and died a few days later. Two boys were in a chapel on Saturday without permission; they put bread on the sacrament trays and were running up and down the aisles; one of them looked down and discovered the bread had turned black. In 1860 Brigham Young dedicated "Salem Pond," a new irrigation project, and promised that no one would die in the pond if the people refrained from swimming on Sunday; the eight people who have since drowned there were all swimming on Sunday. In southern Utah, a young man refused a mission call; about a month later he died in an automobile crash. In Springville not long ago three boys took a ouija board to the cemetery on Halloween night and asked it when they would die; within three years, in accordance with the ouija board's answer, all three were dead, one from suicide and two from accidents.

In no place do these stories flourish as abundantly as they do in the mission field. They are told over and over again to impress on the missionaries the sacredness of their callings and to demonstrate that the power of the priesthood is not to be tampered with. According to one story, a photograph taken of an elder in swimming, against mission rules, showed an evil-looking form hovering over his head. A story from Brazil tells of a missionary who refused to sleep in his garments at night because of the hot, humid weather: "When his companion woke in the morning he found the errant elder pressed into the wall so hard that he could hardly pull him off. The elder was obviously dead from being thus mashed into the wall." One of the most widely known stories, recounted in practically every mission, tells of elders who, as in the following account, are struck dead for testing their priesthood power by attempting to ordain a post or a coke bottle or an animal: "Two missionaries were messing around, and they decided to confer the Priesthood on a dog which they saw on the street. Before they could complete the ordinance, a bolt of lightning came and struck the dog and the two elders, and it zapped them."

One of the most frightening cycles of stories is that which tells of missionaries who seek a testimony by going through the back door--that is, by seeking first a testimony of the devil. The following story is typical:

> I heard from one of my companions about a particular individual that decided that he would gain his testimony by finding out about the adversary. And so he decided that he would pray to the devil and pray for a manifestation or a vision of some type . . . . As he proceeded to pray, hour after hour, his companion had gone to bed and left him in the middle of the room on his knees, praying for a manifestation, or waiting to see the devil in person. And so, as the story goes, he finally reached the point where he woke, or he made enough noise so his companion woke and went to the window and saw a black figure on a black horse coming down the road towards their apartment. And they were up at least two stories, and this particular individual, as the story goes, jumped out of the window.

Another version of the same story ends a little differently:

> He [the companion] looks over to the bed where his companion has gone to bed finally, and he's completely white and obviously dead from his appearance, and there's a black figure on a white horse in the room, who is laughing. And then it just kind of fades away, until there's nothing. And the companion's dead.

In many versions, the nonpraying companion summons the mission president for help. Usually when they enter the room by breaking down the door they find the praying elder suspended in the air, his hair sometimes as white as an old man's. In one account, when they open the door, the suspended elder's body is slammed against the wall, instant death the result. In another they find the bed pinned to the ceiling with the missionary dead between bed and ceiling. In still another the elder is in bed, burned from one end to the other.

These stories do not make pleasant reading, nor telling. Anyone who doubts their evocative power need only sit in his office late at night, as I have done, listening to them on tape. I think I can say with some assurance that a group of missionaries sitting up telling the stories would not lightly dishonor their priesthood for some time to come. From these stories, unpleasant though they may be, we find good examples of how folklore controls behavior, molding it, in this instance through tales of horror, to fit the accepted norms of the group.

Most Mormon folklore is not so dark and gloomy as these devil stories. Much of it, indeed, suggests that God is in his heaven and that all is right with the world--or, at least, that all <u>will</u> be right with the world. Committed to a messianic view of life, most of us are convinced that if we will only endure to the end we will win in the end. Yet, as turmoil and unrest swirl around us, it is difficult at times not to feel, with Arnold, that

> . . . we are here as on a darkling plain
> Swept with confused alarms of struggle and flight,
> Where ignorant armies clash by night.12

But our folklore persuades us otherwise. It teaches us that there is, after all, order in the universe and that if things get too much out of hand, God will step in and set them right.

Consider, for example, the following story:

> There was war between the Arabs and the Jews and the Jews were out-numbered by hundreds, thousands. They had one cannon and they had like about ten men, and the Arabs had stuff from Russia, artillery and all sorts of stuff. And the Jews were banging on cans and moving the cannon over here and they'd shoot it and then they'd move it back and shoot it so the Arabs would think they had lots of men. And they were only fooled for a little while.
> And then when the Jews had just about run out of all their ammo and they were ready to surrender, then the Arabs, they all threw down their weapons and came walking and waving the white flag and everything, surrendering to these Jews. And the Jews walk out and there's ten of them. And the Arab guy who was spokesman for the group said: "Where are those thousands of troops that were just

> across the hill with the man in white leading them? This man was dressed in white and he was leading all these thousands of men and he had a long beard."

In some accounts three men with white flowing beards appear to the Arab generals and warn them to surrender or to face annihilation. The story, one of the most popular Nephite accounts to develop in recent years,[13] has been attached to all the Arab-Israeli wars: the 1948 War, the 1956 War, and 1967 War, and the recent war that brought about our oil crisis. It persuades those who believe it that God's plans for the Jews will not be thwarted and that he will not allow the wrong side to win in the Middle East.

On a less grand but no less significant scale we hear stories which convince us that the missionary system will succeed in taking the gospel to the world. For example, a recent story tells of a missionary in the Language Training Mission who had gotten up one hot night to take a shower:

> He took his shower and returned or began to return to his room. Halfway down the hall he stopped because he heard a noise and wheeled around. Upon doing so he saw before each door an armed guard. Each one was a full six feet six inches tall, and regally dressed as one might expect a Nephite army to be dressed. One sees many such pictures of Moroni. Each one was standing at attention, and the ones at the end of the hall behind him were changing guard, therefore the noise.

From the mission fields come numerous accounts of these guardian warriors being put to good service. Missionaries are saved from storms, rescued from violent mobs, and pulled from flaming wrecks on the freeway. In one instance, two lady missionaries who run out of gasoline in the middle of a New Mexico desert fortuitously discover a service station, fill up, and proceed on their journey; on their next trip over the same road they learn that no station has ever existed at the place where they filled their car with gas. After being badly treated on one street in Taiwan, the missionaries shake dust from their feet and the entire street burns down. In South America the elders dust their feet and a town is destroyed by wind. Two elders leave their garments at a laundry, and when the proprietor holds them up for ridicule, both he and the laundry burn, the fire so hot, in one instance, that it melts the bricks.

With the monstrous Texas murders fresh in our minds and with other stories of opposition to the missionary program familiar to us all, we take comfort in stories that testify that the missionary system, and with it the gospel, will prevail and that our righteous sons and daughters will be protected from harm. The stories thus provide their listeners a sense of security and equilibrium in an unsure world.

In discussing the contribution of myth and ritual to the stability of a society, anthropologist Radcliffe-Brown has argued that members of society share a "system of sentiments" about right and wrong and about the order of the universe and that it is the continuance of these collective sentiments that makes the survival of society possible. The function of folklore is, he says, through "regular and adequate expression," to keep these sentiments alive in the minds of the people.[14] All the examples I have given above fit Radcliffe-Brown's formula rather neatly. They reinforce our belief in Church dogma and practice; they persuade us to follow accepted standards of behavior by showing what will happen to us if we do and, particularly, what will happen to us if we don't; and they give rest to our souls by showing that there is order and purpose in the universe. But in all the examples I have given, I have left out one very important person--J. Golden Kimball.

How do we deal with J. Golden Kimball? More important, how do we deal with the fact that thirty-seven years after his death Mormons still tell more anecdotes about him than about any other figure in Church history? At first brush, the stories told about him certainly seem not to fit Radcliffe-Brown's model. They often make fun of Church practice. They do not give one a particularly strong feeling for the cosmic order of things. And they inspire correct behavior only in the sense that those who tell the stories fear they may be struck dead for doing so.

To answer this question about the J. Golden Kimball stories, let us look briefly at a missionary tale. By far the best-known and most popular story my colleague John B. Harris and I have collected in our study of missionary lore tells of a pair of enterprising elders who, deciding to take an unauthorized trip, make their weekly activity reports out three months in advance, leave them with their landlady with instructions to send one in each week to the mission office, and then leave on an unearned vacation. A few weeks before their return, the landlady mixes up the reports, sends one in out of sequence, and they are caught. The place of the unauthorized trip (New York, the Riviera, Cairo, Moscow, the Easter Islands, the bush country of Australia) varies greatly; otherwise, the details of the story, known in virtually every mission, are the same.

One could argue that, since the wayward elders are always caught, the story serves as a warning to obey mission rules. Perhaps it does. But most missionaries enjoy the story because they find it amusing. One returned missionary who had served as assistant to the mission president told me: "You would always like to do something like that yourself, and you kinda admire someone who has the guts to do it." In other words the hero in this story does for the missionary what he is not allowed to do himself--travel more than five kilometers beyond the boundaries of his assigned city.

Folklorists have long been intrigued by the problem we face here: Why do characters in traditional narratives commit acts that the tellers of the tales cannot, or ought not, commit themselves? The answer seems to be, as the comment of my returned-missionary friend suggests, that folklore as a mirror for culture reveals not only outward behavior but also inner desires, not only what we can do but also what we might like to do if society did not decree otherwise.

Speaking on this issue, Roger Abrahams has argued that hero stories project cultural values in two ways: "as a guide for future action in real life and as an expression of dream-life, of wish-fulfillment." Of this second kind of projection, he says:

> In many groups there is a trickster hero who expends much of his energy in anti-social or anti-authoritarian activity. Even when this results in benefits to the group, his actions can not be interpreted as providing a model for future conduct. He is a projection of desires generally thwarted by society. His celebrated deeds function as an approved steam-valve for the group; he is allowed to perform in this basically childish way so that the group may vicariously live his adventures without actually acting on his impulses. To encourage such action would be to place the existence of the group in jeopardy.[15]

Applied to the J. Golden Kimball cycle, Abrahams's dictum means that the stories provide us the pleasure of sin without the need of suffering its consequences. More seriously, they contribute to the social cohesion Radcliffe-Brown talks about by making it easier for us to live with societal pressures that inhibit our natural inclinations and might otherwise be the undoing of both ourselves and our society.

In this connection, we should remember that the J. Golden Kimball stories are, in the final analysis, no longer about J.

Golden Kimball at all. They are about us. We are the ones who keep them alive by continual retelling and by continual reshaping. We should be concerned, I believe, not so much with trying to characterize Kimball but rather with trying to understand ourselves--trying to understand why we have created the kind of character who lives in the legend, and trying to discover what need the telling of the stories fills in our own lives.

I believe it is a need to assert one's own personality and to resist, or at least to deflate, those who exercise authority over us. One of my friends, for instance, says he takes delight in the J. Golden Kimball stories because he believes reverence for people is absurd and because J. Golden is always putting down the revered. Those who would like to censor the stories because of their colorful language have really missed their best argument. If the stories are dangerous, they are so not because of their language but because of their expressed disrespect for authority. In joke after joke, J. Golden is juxtaposed alongside a higher, more sour and dour authority. In almost every instance he lets the air out of this authority and gets away with it.

For example:

> J. Golden was talking with one of the Quorum members one time and the "brother" said to him: "Brother Kimball, I don't see how you can swear so much. Why I'd rather commit adultery than swear so much." J. Golden answered, "Wouldn't we all, brother? Wouldn't we all?"

Another story states:

> This happened in St. George. J. Golden was down there with an Apostle for stake conference. J. Golden fell asleep while the Apostle was talking and fell off his chair right at the feet of the Apostle. The Apostle looked rather strongly at Brother Kimball, who responded: "Well, you shouldn't be so damn boring."

Most of us know the story of how President Grant insisted on writing J. Golden's conference address because he had lost confidence in the crusty old man's ability to speak without swearing. J. Golden took the talk as he walked toward the podium, stared at President Grant's handwriting, then screeched over the microphone: "Good hell, Hebe, I can't read a damn word of this." There is humor, of course, in the swearing and in the thwarting of President Grant's plan, but the real laughter is evoked by the word "Hebe." Prophet, seer, and revelator--yes. But never Hebe. Therein lies the sacrilege.

Though the J. Golden Kimball accounts are the best known, they are by no means the only stories that put down authority figures. A large number of "Mormon bishop" jokes also serve this end. For example:

> This bishop lost his bicycle and suspected that it was stolen, so he talked with his counselors about it and asked them to help him find out who stole it. The bishop decided to give a little talk in church about the ten commandments, and when he came to the commandment about "Thou shalt not steal," he would slow down and pause so that his counselors could see who squirmed and find out who it was that stole his bicycle. Well, the bishop got up in church and started preaching about the ten commandments, but when he came to the commandment about stealing he didn't even slow down. He just rattled right on and didn't even pause at all. Afterwards his counselors asked him why he didn't slow down so they could see who squirmed when he talked about stealing. The bishop said, "Well, when I came to the commandment 'Thou shalt not commit adultery' I remembered where I left my bicycle."[16]

It is interesting to note that not only is the bishop in this joke made to look ridiculous; he is made so by violation of the very law that bishops are usually most diligent to enforce among their charges.

Even among our children the tendency to rebel against authority by using folklore is sometimes evident. Fed a diet of saccharine-sweet songs by solicitous Primary and Sunday School teachers, youngsters often respond with parodies like the following:

> I have five little fingers on one little hand;
> I have six little fingers on my other hand.
> During all the long hours till daylight is through,
> I have one little finger with nothing to do.

Some of the jokes project not just a resistance to authority, but also a concern with certain church practices. For example:

> One day Saint Peter was repairing the Gates of Heaven and a Catholic priest who had just died came to get in.
> "It'll be a few minutes before you can enter," Saint Peter said. "The gates are broken. You can go over there and have a cup of coffee while you wait."
> The priest calmly began drinking his coffee and Saint Peter returned to his work. Not long after, a Protestant minister who had just died approached Saint Peter to enter heaven.
> "You'll have to wait while I fix these gates," Saint Peter said. "Just go over there and have some coffee."
> The minister joined the priest. Soon a Mormon bishop who had just died came up to Saint Peter and wanted to get into heaven.
> Saint Peter said, "You'll have to go to hell. I don't have time to make hot chocolate."

A joke which made the rounds about three months ago tells that

> President Kimball sent out messages for all members of the church to meet on temple square for an important message. The tabernacle, the Assembly Hall, and the Salt Palace were full, and people were all over. President Kimball got up and said: "Saints, I've got some good news and some bad news. First the good news. We have just received a telegram from Western Union; the Millenium is here. Christ arrives in two days. Now for the bad news. We're all supposed to meet at the Vatican."

Some Mormons are offended by this story because we haven't the necessary psychic distance to tell jokes about a living head of the Church the way we can tell them, for instance, about Brigham Young. But the story itself is relatively innocent, spoofing the belief that only Mormons will make it to heaven. Other jokes are much more serious. Just after Joseph Fielding Smith became President of the Church, I heard the following story:

> Before President McKay died, Jessie Evans Smith used to get her husband out of bed each morning and say: "All right, Joseph, it's time for our exercises. Ready. One, two, three. Outlive David O.; outlive David O.

For me this joke goes beyond the bounds of reasonable propriety. Because I have been taught so long and so well to honor the prophet, I cannot hear it with pleasure. But it is there, and it cannot be ignored. It reflects the concerns of some Mormons that ascendancy to the Presidency seems to result from longevity rather than from revelation and that we are forever destined to be led by men long past their prime.

The stories we have been considering here suggest that however willingly we live under our authoritarian system we do not always do so easily. If the jokes trouble us, we should remember the point made by Abrahams: jokes like these do not provide models for conduct; they provide instead a means of easing the pressures developed by the system we live under. And no matter what system we live under there will be pressures. We should also remember that the people who tell these jokes are not out to overthrow the system. They are simply finding release from their frustrations through laughter. Next Sunday will find most of them in church faithfully attending their duties. The fact that they are there may indeed be a result of their saving sense of humor.

These stories, then, like the stories of divine intervention in the affairs of man, contribute to the stability of both the Church and its members. And herein lies the paradox of Mormon folklore: On the one hand, it persuades members to accept and support Church dogma and practice; on the other, it provides them with the means of coming to terms with the tensions such support at times imposes upon them.

In conclusion, and in answer again to Richard Anderson's questions, Mormon folklore is Mormon literature--folk literature. The materials of this literature are not some sort of fossilized artifacts surviving from an earlier period and valuable only to the curio-collecting antiquarian. They are instead a body of living traditions constantly renewed and constantly re-created as Mormons react to the circumstances of their contemporary environment. This material is valuable to the student of Mormon culture because it gives him keen insight into the Mormon mind and a better understanding of Mormon behavior. It is valuable to the people themselves because it reaffirms their conviction in the truthfulness of the gospel; it inspires them to conform to accepted patterns of behavior;

it persuades them that God is on their side and in times of trouble will come to their aid; and, finally, when the burdens of their religion at times weigh too heavily upon them, it provides them with the means to ease the pressure by laughing at both themselves and the system and thus to face the new day with equanimity.

REFERENCES

1. The term folklore was coined by William John Thoms in a letter to The Athenaeum, 982(22 August 1846):862-63. Thoms, writing under the name Ambrose Merton, suggested that this "good Saxon compound" replace the term popular antiquities then in vogue. For definitions of folklore given by twenty-one twentieth-century scholars, see Funk & Wagnalls Standard Dictionary of Folklore, Mythology, and Legend, ed. Maria Leach, 1(New York, 1949):398-403. For a recent appraisal of folklore study, see Toward New Perspectives in Folklore, ed. Richard Bauman, special issue of Journal of American Folklore, 84 (1971).

2. Letter from Joseph Fielding Smith to Hector Lee, 15 December 1941, printed by Lee in "The Three Nephites: The Substance and Significance of the Legend in Folklore," diss., University of New Mexico, 1947, p. 217.

3. Unless otherwise noted, all items of Mormon folklore discussed in this paper, as well as comments of informants, are located in the Brigham Young University Folklore Archives, c/o English Department.

4. Austin E. Fife, "The Legend of the Three Nephites among the Mormons," Journal of American Folklore, 53(1940):27-29.

5. The same individual will often tell the same story quite differently, depending on his reasons for telling it and upon his audience. For example, I have two versions of the James Rencher story told by the same informant, one with the political theme and one without it. In the first instance, the informant focuses on politics because he wants to persuade the students in his religion class that the general authorities have the right to speak out on political issues.

6. Brigham Young University Library, Manuscript Collection, M884.

7. The First Presidency first addressed the issue in a letter (30 March 1970) mailed to stake presidents, mission presidents, and bishops. The letter was reprinted in the Church News, 4 April 1970.

8. N. Scott Momaday, "The Man Made of Words," Brigham Young University Forum Address, 14 January 1975.

9. Cotton Mather, Magnalia Christi Americana: Or, the Ecclesiastical History of New-England (1702), 2 vols. (Hartford, 1853), 2:362.

10. Richard Cracroft and Neal E. Lambert, A Believing People: Literature of the Latter-day Saints (Provo, Utah: Brigham Young University Press, 1974), p. 3.

11. For a brief discussion of this version of the story, see Jan Harold Brunvand, "Modern Legends of Mormondom, or, Supernaturalism is Alive and Well in Salt Lake City," in American Folk Legend: A Symposium, ed. Wayland D. Hand (Berkeley, Los Angeles, and London, 1971), p. 200.

12. Matthew Arnold, "Dover Beach," in The Poems of Matthew Arnold, 1840-1867 (London, 1926), p. 402.

13. This story seems to have entered the Nephite tradition from printed sources. A somewhat different version from the one given here was cited by Joseph Fielding Smith in The Signs of the Times (Salt Lake City, 1952), pp. 227-29. Two years later LeGrand Richards printed the same story in Israel, Do You Know? (Salt Lake City, 1954), pp. 229-33. Both President Smith and Elder Richards cited as their source an article in The Jewish Hope by Arthur U. Michelson. Neither of them argued that the men in the story were Nephites but merely suggested that they might have been.

14. A. R. Radcliffe-Brown, "The Interpretation of Andamanese Customs and Beliefs: Myths and Legends," in The Andaman Islanders (Cambridge, 1922), pp. 376-405.

15. Roger D. Abrahams, "Some Varieties of Heroes in America," Journal of the Folklore Institute, 3(1966):341-42.

16. Many stories like this one are Mormon not by birth but by adoption. They have come originally from the large body of anticlerical stories known throughout much of the world. Within the Church they are adapted to fit the framework of Mormon culture.

SOC
F
591
E8223

DATE DUE	
~~DEC 15 79~~	
ILL GRANT ~~MAY 28 1993~~	